the infinite light

A book about God

Aryeh Kaplan

Published by the National Conference of Synagogue
Youth/Union of Orthodox Jewish Congregations of America,
333 Seventh Avenue, New York, NY 10001.

Distributed by Mesorah Publications, Inc., 4401 Second Avenue,
Brooklyn, NY 11232. Distributed in Israel by Sifriati/A. Gitler
Books, 4 Bilu Street, P.O.B. 14075, Tel Aviv 61140. Distributed in
Europe by J. Lehmann Hebrew Booksellers, 20 Cambridge
Terrace, Gateshead, Tyne & Wear, England NE8 1RP.

ISBN 1-879016-19-2

PRINTED IN THE UNITED STATES OF AMERICA

THE INFINITE LIGHT

Table of Contents

Publication of this volume was made possible
in substantial part by a generous contribution from
Mrs. Nathalie Kunen
and the Kaye, Scholer, Fierman, Hayes and Handler
Mishnah Club
in memory of Milton Kunen.

Milton Kunen was a scholar of the law
—both secular and talmudic—
and, most significantly, a lover of learning.
This book is a fitting memorial
to the ideal exemplified by his life.

INTRODUCTION

"The Infinite Light", A Book about G-d

The first man was speechless when confronted by the divine question, Where are you? We, his descendants are inarticulate in our response to man's question, Where is G-d?

Achieving an awareness of G-d is a difficult task. The pursuit of that awareness involves relentless study and questioning, as well as mitzvah observance and Torah living. As Jews, we do not rely on dreams and heavenly manifestations to actualize G-d's presence in our lives. The true appreciation of a purposeful, personal G-d can only derive from a purposeful life lived in accordance with a purposeful creation.

The first human being to recognize the existence of G-d through his own observation was Abraham. Some commentaries say that this spectacular feat was accomplished at the age of forty-six, when his mental powers had attained their greatest acuity. Others maintain that it was at the age of three that Abraham experienced the original, auto-induced personal revelation.

Rabbi Menachem Mendel of Kotzk explains that even according to the former opinion, Abraham's first 46 years were not wasted on the impotent emptiness of idolatry. They were years of searching, of questioning, of delving into the mysteries of human and universal existence. When at age 46, Abraham achieved the pinnacle of man's sensitivity to creation, it was not a thunderclap, not an apparition that preceded this discovery but rather the calm, steady reflection of Abraham's magnificent mind and gigantic spirit.

It is instructive that it was Abraham, the paragon of righteousness in human affairs, who was privileged to be the first to recognize G-d, and to understand His concern for human behavior.

In contemporary society, particularly among young people we sense a not quite conscious stirring, a movement within humanity, which searches and strives for meaning in life. Logotherapy, a school of psychodynamics, projects "meaning" as the central idea of human existence. There is a sense that man cannot achieve happiness purely through satisfaction of material goals. The high statistics of suicide in developed countries, as well as the almost universal statement that "life seemed meaningless" by attempted suicides, attest to this fact.

Ultimately, searching for meaning is striving for G-d. This book was conceived as an atlas to aid the searching Jew, in mapping his personal journey in the quest for the ultimate meaning of human existence, the knowledge of G-d. The author draws from the entire spectrum of our tradition to present an understanding of G-d, his Torah, and of Man's duty to observe the truths embodied in it.

Rabbi Judah Halevi once wrote "If I were to see Him in a dream, I would continue to sleep forever". We present this work in the hope that it will enable us to better see Him in our lives to that we may indeed seize our portion of eternity.

Kislev 6, 5740
November 26, 1979

Baruch Taub

PART ONE

FOUNDATIONS

In order to speak about Judaism, we must speak about man and about life in general. Judaism is, first of all, a way of life, and its depth touches upon the very foundations of human existence. If you truly understand Judaism, you know the ultimate secret of life's purpose.

One of the most important elements of life is purpose. There is an old song that asks, "Why was I born, why am I living? What do I get, what am I giving?" These are questions that man has been asking himself every since he first began using his mind.

Have you ever stopped and asked yourself such questions?

Why was I born?

What meaning does my life have?

Why am I myself?

How should I live this one life of mine?

What do I have to offer life?

When we are young, such questions often bother us. Among the problems of growing up, we try to find a philosophy of life to follow. But then, caught in the business world, the market place, and the toil of raising a family, we often forget these questions. And sometimes we are rudely awakened. When tragedy strikes, the questions are thrown at us like buckets of ice water. When we grow old—and we all do grow old—we may gaze back at a lifetime and wonder, "What did I live for?"

We have but one life and must make the most of it. We all want to do what is "right." We want somehow to justify our lives. Rare indeed is the person who can say, *"This is wrong, but I will do it anyway."*

We all have a feeling that some things are right and others are wrong. We have a feeling that there is meaning to life. But many of us go no further. Even when we ask the questions, we do not go very far in seeking answers.

A very wise man once said, "The unexamined life is not worth living."

People can spend their lives seeking pleasure, fame and riches, and never once stop to ask themselves if these things are really important. But unless one gives this serious thought, he will never know whether or not he is doing the right thing. He may spend his entire life pursuing useless and even dangerous goals.

The most fundamental principal of Judaism is the realization that the universe is purposeful, and that man has a purpose in life.[1]

Our sages thus teach us, "A person must have the wisdom . . . to know why he is and why he exists. He must look back at his life, and realize where he is going."[2]

Both man and nature have purpose because they were created by a purposeful Being. We call this Being God.[3]

It is impossible to imagine the world as having purpose without a Creator. Without God, the universe would be purposeless and human existence pointless. All life would be completely without meaning or hope.

For the sake of argument, let us look at the negative viewpoint more closely. Let us look at the world through the eyes of a man without belief and see it as the absolute atheist would. Since his world has no purposeful Creator, there is no purpose in existence. Mankind becomes nothing more than an accident, with no more consequence than a bacterium or a stone. Man can even be looked upon as a vile infection and a disease on the surface of this planet.

If there is no purpose to existence, all our hopes, desires and aspirations are nothing more than the mechanizations of the molecules and cells of our brain. We would have no alternative than to agree with a noted cynic who declared, "Man is a sick fly, taking a dizzy ride on a gigantic flywheel."

In a world without purpose, there can be neither good nor evil, since both of these concepts imply purpose. Without a belief in some ultimate purpose, all values become completely subjective, subject to the whim of the individual. Morality becomes a matter of convenience, to be discarded when it does not serve one's immediate goal. One's philosophy of life can simply be, "If you can get away with it, do it."

If existence has neither purpose, meaning nor depth, our attitude toward the world, toward our fellow man, and toward society in general need be little more than "so what."

If there is no God, there is no purpose. And if there is no purpose, all man's endeavors are in vain. The Psalmist alludes to this, when he says, "If God does not build the house, in vain do the builders toil; If God does not watch the city, in vain do the sentries wake" (*Psalms 127:1*).

But we can also look at the other side of the question and gaze at the world through the eyes of true faith. If we believe in God as Creator of the universe, then creation has a mighty purpose and life has an infinitude of depth. If man is to find meaning in life, he must seek God's purpose in creation and spend his days trying to fulfill it. The existence of man, a creature who can search for purpose in life, is no longer a mere accident, but the most significant phenomenon in all creation. The concepts of good and evil take on awesome proportions. That which is in accordance with God's purpose is good, while thwt which goes against it is evil. We are nothing less than partners with God in fulfilling His purpose.

Deep down, no one really feels that everything is meaningless. But many of us lose sight of the true Root of all meaning, often hiding behind a facade of cliches and excuses. Deep down, however, all of us know that there is purpose in life, and ultimately, in all creation.

The old fashioned materialist who was convinced that human life was without goal or purpose and that man is an irresponsible particle of matter engulfed in a maelstrom of meaningless forces, was a man without wisdom. A great philosopher once summed up the folly of this way of thinking by saying, "People who spend their lives with the purpose of proving that it is purposeless, constitute an interesting subject of study."

The Bible flatly says that the nonbeliever is a fool. The Psalmist thus said, "The fool says in his heart, there is no God" (*Psalms 14:1*).

What the Bible is saying is that one who does not believe is both stupid and blind. He does not see what there is to see. Not only is he blind, but he is also likely to act blindly. He does not recognize any purpose in existence, and is therefore likely to act without direction. He does not recognize Truth, and is apt to do everything wrong. He is so unperceptive that he cannot be trusted. He says that there is no God because he is a fool. He is too blind to see God all around him; or else he is too selfish to share his own world with its Creator.

In the entire Bible, you will not find a single philosophical argument for the existence of God. It is simply assumed. The Bible does not waste time trying to convice the atheist that he is wrong. He is considered a fool, too dull to understand, or too wicked to want to.

Belief, like beauty, is in the eye of the beholder. For over three thousand years, the existence of God was self-evident to the Jew. He needed no proof or demonstration.

The very existence of a universe implied a creator. The Psalmist thus said, "The heavens declare the glory of God, and the skies proclaim His handiwork" (*Psalms 19:2*). Their very existence is a hymn, declaring the glory of their Creator.[5]

The Prophet speaks of this most lucidly when he says (*Isaiah 40:21, 26*):

> Do you not know?
>> Have you not heard?
> Was it not told to you from the beginning?
>> Do you not understand how the earth was founded?

. . .

> Lift up your eyes to the stars
>> And see Who has created them
> He numbers them all like an army,
>> He calls them all by name . . .

2.

There is a legend that throws much light on this subject:[6]

A philosopher once came to Rabbi Meir and told him, "I don't believe in God. I feel that the universe came into being by itself, of its own accord, without any outside help."

Rabbi Meir did not reply. A few days later, he came to the philosopher, and showed him a beautiful piece of poetry, written in a find hand on smooth white parchment.

The philosopher looked at the parchment and admired it. He asked, "Who is the great poet who wrote this lovely poem? Who was the talented scribe who copied it?"

Rabbi Meir shook his head and answered, "You are completely wrong. There was no poet. There was no scribe. This is what really happened. The parchment was lying on my desk next to a bottle of ink. A cat accidently knocked over the bottle, spilling ink all over the parchment. This poem was the result."

The philosopher looked at Rabbi Meir in amazement. He said, "But that is impossible! Such a lovely poem! Such perfect script! Such things do not come into being by themselves. There must be an author! There must be a scribe!"

Rabbi Meir smiled. He answered the philosopher, "You yourself have said it! How could the universe, which is much more beautiful than any poem, come into being by itself? There must be an Author. There must be a Creator."

What Rabbi Meir was dramatizing, of course, was the argument from design. We see a world that appears to be well planned and purposeful. Everything in nature fits into its place. Tremendously complex creatures, such as man himself, exist in this world. How can a sane man really believe that all of this came into being without a purposeful Creator?

There is a Midrash telling us that this is how Abraham first realized the existence of God. Abraham said, "Is it possible that a brightly illuminated castle can exist without an owner? Can one say that this world exists without a Creator?"[7]

Ultimately, there is a certain blindness involved in not seeing God. This is what the Prophet meant when he said (*Isaiah 29:16*):

How upside down are things!
Is the potter no better than the clay?
Can something say of its maker,
"He did not make me"?
Can a pot say of the potter,
"He has no skill"?

All that we must do is ask the right questions. The *Zohar*[8] quotes the verse, "Lift up your eyes to the stars, and see, *Who* has created *these*?" (*Isaiah 40:26*). The world that we see is *these*, *Eleh* in Hebrew. Look at *these*, and ask *Who*—*Mi* in Hebrew. Combine the two words, *Eleh* and *Mi*—these and Who—and you obtain *Elohim*—the Hebrew name for God. One must merely ask the right questions, and God appears in the answers.

A person need only look at himself, and he will see the handiwork of the Creator. The fact that you can think, or move your hand, is the greatest miracle possible. The Psalmist recognized this when he exclaimed, "I will thank God, for I am fearfully and wonderfully made" (*Psalms 139:14*).

All of this is summed up in one sentence in the Bible: "From my flesh, I will see God" (*Job 19:26*).[9] I can see God in the very fact that something as miraculous as my flesh can exist.

3.

It is told that King Frederic the Great once asked his Lutheran pastor to provide him with a visible proof of God's existence. The pastor answered with just two words: The Jews.

For the Jew, the question of God's existence is no mere philosophical exercise. It is linked to our very history. We have seen the rise of the Babylonians, the Persians, the Phoenicians, the Hittites, the Philistines, the Greeks and the Romans, all the great nations of the pagan era, and we have also witnessed their fall. All these great civilizations were born, reached maturity, and died. This is the pattern of history. All the great civilizations of antiquity have passed on. There is but one exception, and we are still reading and writing books.

We have a long history of miraculous survival and continuous growth. Our people have lived through four thousand years of persecution, enslavement, slaughter, exile, torture, inquisition, pogrom and death camp. We were enslaved by the Egyptians, slaughtered by the Philistines, exiled by the Babylonians, dispersed by the Romans, and butchered and chased from land to land in Europe. But miracle of miracles, we are still here today.

There is absolutely no theory of history that can explain this in a natural manner. Social scientists may find many unusual records of survival among various peoples of the world, but nothing even comes remotely close to the story of the Jew.

The Midrash[10] tells us that the Roman emperor Hadrian once remarked to Rabbi Joshua, "Great indeed must be the lamb, Israel, that it can survive among seventy wolves." Rabbi Joshua replied, "Great is the Shepherd, Who rescues her and protects her."

We are all familiar with the song in the Passover Hagaddah, where this theme is repeated:[11]

> This is what has stood up
>   for our fathers and for us:
> Not one alone
>   has stood up to finish us,
> But in every generation
>   they rise to finish us;
> But God, blessed be He,
>   saves us from their hand!

This great miracle of Jewish survival cannot be without meaning. It is something that is unique in the annals of history. If you want to see a real miracle, just look into a mirror. One of the greatest possible miracles is the fact that after four thousand years, there is still such a thing as a Jew.

God told us through His prophet, "You are My witnesses, says the Lord, and I am God" (*Isaiah 43:12*). The Midrash states that God is known as such in the world because we bear witness to Him.[12] In a sense, our very existence and survival bear witness to God.

4.

It is our history that defines our relationship with God and makes Judaism unique among world religions.

Once we see God as Creator, it is obvious that His creation has purpose. It should also be obvious that He would eventually reveal this purpose to man. We believe that this took place at Mount Sinai.

To understand our reason for this belief, we must see how Judaism differs from all other religions.

Other religions begin with a single individual. He claims to have a special message, and gradually gathers a following. His followers spread the word and gather converts, and a new religion is born. Virtually every world religion follows this pattern.

The one exception is Judaism.

God gathered an entire people, three million strong,[13] to the foot of Mount Sinai, and proclaimed His message. Every man, woman and child heard God's voice, proclaiming the Ten Commandments. Thus was a bond forged between God and Israel.[14]

This was an event unique in the history of mankind. It remained imprinted deeply in the Jewish soul throughout all of our history. It was something that was not to be forgotten.

The Torah thus tells us, "Be most careful, and watch yourself, that you not forget the things that you saw with your own eyes. Do not let them pass from your minds as long as you live. Teach them to your children, and to your children's children: The day when you stood before God. . . ." (*Deuteronomy 4:9–10*). This is stated in the most emphatic terms, and there are some who count it among the commandments of the Torah.[15]

The revelation at Sinai came just seven weeks after another unique event in Jewish history. This was the Exodus from Egypt. God revealed Himself to an entire people and literally changed the course of both nature and history. Here too was an event unique in the history of mankind.[16]

The Torah itself speaks of this when it says "Did God ever venture to take a nation to Himself from another nation, with a challenge, with signs and wonders, as the Lord your God did in Egypt, before your very eyes. You have had sure proof that the Lord is God, there is no other" (*Deuteronomy 4:34*).

There may be other religions in the world, but none had the powerful beginning of Judaism. It is the Exodus that makes us unique.

The Exodus not only made us uniquely aware of God, but it also showed Him to be profoundly involved in the affairs of man.

The Torah warns us never to forget the Exodus. We thus find, "Beware, that you not forget God, Who brought you out of the land of Egypt, from the house of slavery" (*Deuteronomy 6:12*). There are some who count this among the commandments of the Torah.[17]

The impact of the Exodus remained imprinted on the Jewish mind throughout our history. We saw every persecutor as Pharaoh, with God standing on the sidelines, ready to repeat the miracle of the Exodus. This, in part, accounts for the miracle of our survival.

5.

In giving the Ten Commandments, God opened with the words "I am the Lord your God, Who took you out of the land of Egypt, from the house of slavery" (*Exodus 20:2*)[18]

There are some commentators who ask why God mentioned the Exodus, rather than the more universal fact that He is Creator of the universe.[19] In other words, why did He not say, "I am the Lord your God, Creator of heaven and earth"?

They answer that this is because the latter statement would allow us to make a serious mistake. We could erroneously think of God as Creator, and yet believe that He has no interest in the affairs of man.[20]

In the opening words of the Ten Commandments, God was telling us that He *is* involved in the affairs of man, and has a profound interest in everything we do. God gave the Exodus as an example, for it was here that the entire Jewish people experienced Him. To them, God was no mere philosophical abstraction. They actually saw His deeds, and were aware of Him to such an extent that they were able to point and say, "This is my God."[21]

One who does not accept the fact that God is involved and interested in our affairs and actions cannot be said to believe. He may claim to believe in God, but it is not the God of Israel. As such, he is considered a nonbeliever.[22]

We believe in God, both as the God of creation and as the God of history. Judaism totally rejects the deistic concept of a God who created the world and then abandoned it with neither ruler, guide nor judge. Our sages teach us that one who says "there is neither Judge nor judgment" is considered a nonbeliever.[23] It is of such people that the Prophet was speaking when he exclaimed "They say: God does not see, God has forsaken the earth" (*Ezekiel 8:12*).

The entire history of Judaism bears witness to God's active involvement in the affairs of man. Indeed, this is born out by the history of mankind in general. The experience of men and nations clearly indicates that only good is stable. Evil, on the other hand, always tends to destroy itself.[24] This is what the Bible means when it says, "There are many thoughts in man's heart, but the counsel of God is what stands" (*Proverbs 19:21*).

The first Commandment, "I am the Lord your God," is interpreted by most authorities as an actual commandment to believe in God.[25] As such, it is the first and foremost commandment. Any moment that a person so much as thinks that he believes in God's existence, he is fulfilling this commandment.[26]

There are other authorities, however, who go a step further. They write that belief in God is much too basic a part of Judaism to be a mere commandment.[27] Rather, they see this as an introduction to the commandments, and a statement that forms the very basis of Judaism.

The second of the Ten Commandments tells us, "You shall have no other gods before Me" (*Exodus 20:3*). Essentially, this is a commandment not to believe in any deity other than the One True God, Creator of all things.[28]

Like the first Commandment, this can be fulfilled by mere thought. Thus, a person can fulfill this commandment at any time merely by thinking that he does not believe in any other God.[29] Conversely, one who even thinks and believes any idolatrous idea is guilty of violating this commandment and may be punished accordingly. The Prophet thus said, "These men have set up idols in their hearts" (*Ezekiel 14:3*).[30]

The commandment states, "You shall not have any other gods *before Me*." When God said "before Me," He was stressing that one may not believe in any other deity, even if he also believes in God.[31] One who sets up any mediator between God and man is similarly guilty of violating this commandment.[32]

Let us look into this a bit more closely. If a person believes in G-d, then what need does he have for any other deity? The answer that some non-Jewish thinkers give is that God is so high that He is unapproachable without a mediator. The second commandment teaches us that this, too, is idolatry.

God is infinite. To say that He needs a mediator to hear our prayers is to deny His infinite wisdom.

It is therefore a foundation of our faith to believe that all prayer must be addressed directly to God.[33]

One who calls any other being a god is guilty of idolatry.[34]

Our sages thus teach us, "One who takes God's name in partnership with something else is torn out of this world. It is thus written, 'only to God alone' (*Exodus 22:19*)."[35]

The prohibition against idolatry applies both to Jew and non-Jew alike.[36] Some authorities, however, say that this is only true where an actual act of idolatry is involved.[37] The prohibition against believing in a "partner" or mediator, in this opinion, applies only to the Jew. These codifiers maintain that as long as a non-Jew believes in God, he may also accept another being as a deity or mediator.[38] They cite as evidence for this the passage, "That you not . . . be drawn away, and worship these things, which the Lord your God has allotted to all other peoples . . ." (*Deuteronomy 4:19*).[39] According to this interpretation, the Torah is saying that belief in other deities is permissible to non-Jews as long as they also believe in God. This opinion would hold that Christianity is a permissible religion for non-Jews, and may indeed be a partial fulfillment of God's ultimate purpose.[40] For a Jew, of course, belief in Christianity is not only forbidden, but is in direct conflict with the second of the Ten Commandments. Furthermore, many authorities extend the prohibition against idolatry to forbid even a non-Jew to believe in a mediator between God and man.[41]

God Himself proclaimed the first two of the Ten Commandments to the entire Jewish nation. The first two therefore are given in the first person: "*I* am the Lord" and "You shall have no other gods before *Me*." In these two cases, God Himself is speaking. The following commandments, on the other hand, speak of God in the third person. Thus, the third Commandment says, "You shall not take the name of the Lord your God in vain" (*Exodus 20:7*). Here God is not saying "do not take *My* name in vain." Rather, someone else is speaking of God. Our traditions thus teach us that only the first two of the Ten Commandments were given to the Jewish people directly by God Himself.[42] All the others, however, were transmitted through Moses. Our sages interpret the following passage as speaking of the first two commandments: "God has spoken once, two [commandments] which I heard" (*Psalm 62:12*).[43]

These first two Commandments constitute the very essence of Judaism. If a person denies the existence of God or accepts any other being as a deity, he is denying this essence. Our sages call him a *Kofer BeIkkar*, literally, one who "denies the essence."[44] They further teach us that no man is more rejected by God than the one who rejects Him.[45]

The first five of the Ten Commandments all involve essentials of Judaism. The commandment not to take God's name in vain relates to God's involvement with the world. If one truly believes that God is interested in man's deeds, he cannot openly show Him disrespect. One who grossly disrespects God's name is really demonstrating his lack of belief.[46]

The fourth Commandment, regarding the Sabbath, is also related to our basic beliefs. Keeping the Sabbath is the one act by which we demonstrate our belief in God as Creator of the universe. One who does not keep the Sabbath denies this belief by his actions, and therefore thrusts himself out of the fold of believers in Judaism.[47]

The fifth Commandment tells us to honor our parents, which again touches upon our faith. The sum total of our traditions has been handed down from generation to generation. Unless a bond of trust and respect exists between generations, these traditions cannot endure.[48] Through the traditions handed down from our ancestors, we know about God and His teachings, as the Torah itself says, "Ask your father and he will inform you, your elders, and they will tell you" (*Deuteronomy 32:7*).

6.

Belief in God is the very foundation of Judaism. However, faith is not just the utterance of words. It is firm belief and conviction with mind and heart, to be acted upon through a course prescribed by God.[49] Faith which does not predicate obedience to God is an absurdity.[50]

Speaking about God is very much like speaking about love. One can spend a lifetime speaking and reading about love, and never have the slightest idea of what it is all about. When one actually experiences it, however, lengthy discussions are no longer needed. The same is true of God. One cannot understand Him unless one experiences Him.

The only way to experience God is through the observance and study of our religious teachings. One who does not do this ultimately denies God.[51] On the other hand, if one studies God's teachings and keeps His commandments, he will ultimately find God.[52] Our sages thus teach us that God says, "If they would only abandon Me but keep My Torah, its light would bring them back."[53]

If one ignores God's commandments, he will ultimately also forget God. The Torah therefore warns us, "Beware that you do not forget the Lord your God by not keeping His commandments, His ordinances and His statutes" (*Deuteronomy 8:11*). Some authorities count this warning among the commandments of the Torah.[54]

It is not enough merely to believe. One must actually live in God's presence. This is what the Psalmist meant when he exclaimed, "I have set God before me at all times" (*Psalms 16:8*).[55]

I can gaze at a beautiful sunset and try to describe it. But unless you open your eyes and see it for yourself, my words are in vain. You must see it to understand and appreciate it.

I can describe the most delicious fruit. But you must taste it to understand what I am saying.

The same is true of God. The Psalmist thus says, "Taste and see that God is good, happy is the man who embraces Him" (*Psalms 34:9*).

PART TWO

GOD

1.

What do we know about God?

Mostly, we know about God from our own experiences, both as individuals and as a people. We know Him from such great events as the Exodus and the Revelation at Sinai. We know Him from the many times that He intervened to guide the history and destiny of our people. We know Him from the careers of people who have been touched by Him.

But most of all, most of us know God through our own experiences. There have been times in all our lives when we have felt close to God, or experienced His hand guiding our lives. It is very easy to forget these times, but if we look back and think, we can remember.

We seek God in many ways. We approach Him in prayer. We keep His commandments. We look at the world and stand in awe at His handiwork.

Who at some time has not contemplated nature and stood awestruck, realizing that he is gazing at the handiwork of God? Who at some time has not shared Job's experience, when he exclaims (*Job 12:7-9*):

> Now ask the beasts, they will teach you,
> The birds of the sky, they will tell you;
> Or speak to the earth, it will teach you,
> The fish of the sea, they will tell you;
> Who cannot learn from all these
> That God's hand has done this?
> In His hand is every living soul,
> The breath of all human flesh.

We experience God in our own lives and also know of Him from the history of our ancestors. We therefore call Him, "our God and God of our fathers." He is our God because we ourselves have experienced Him, but He is also God of our fathers, because we know even more about Him from our traditions and history. This is what our people sang at the Red Sea, "This is my God, I will glorify Him; my father's God, I will praise Him" (*Exodus 15:2*).

We know God for His mighty deeds, but also from his small miracles. God fashioned the stars, but He also listens to the cry of the small child. The Psalmist expresses this most beautifully when he says, "He rides upon the skies, His name is God . . . the Father of orphans, the Judge of widows, He is God in His holy place. God gives the friendless a home, and frees the captive, bringing him to safety" (*Psalms 68:5-6*). Our sages thus teach us, "Wherever you find God's greatness, you also find His humility."[1]

We know God as the Highest, and yet, we seek Him with humility. As long as one is filled with his own egotism, he has no room for God. Our sages teach us that God says that He cannot abide in the same world with the haughty man.[2] A man must surrender his own ego before he can truly find God. This is God's message, "I dwell in a high and holy place, but I am with the brokenhearted and humble. I revive the humble spirit and give new life to the broken heart" (*Isaiah 57:15*).

We know God through love. It is He who bids us, "You shall love your neighbor as yourself" (*Leviticus 19:18*). We know of this love as a reflection of our love for God, as the Torah says, "You shall love the Lord your God, with all your heart, with all your soul, and with all your might" (*Deuteronomy 6:5*). We know of His infinite love for us, as He announced through His prophet, "I love you with an infinite world of love, and so, have drawn you to Me with affection" (*C§Jeremiah 31:3*). And there are times when we can say along with the Psalmist, "O God, my God, I seek You, my soul thirsts, my flesh longs for You, like a dry and thirsty land that has no water" (*Psalms 63:2*).

We know God through our hope in the future. We know Him through our prayers for life, health and prosperity. We know Him through our hopes for Israel, for all mankind, for peace and brotherhood among men. We know Him through our optimism that the world will be good in the end.

One of the most profound prayers ever written is the *Amidah* (or *Shemoneh Esreh*), the silent, standing prayer, that every Jew has repeated three times each day for the past 2500 years. In the opening lines of this prayer we express our most basic feelings toward God:

> Blessed are You O Lord,
>> Our God and God of our fathers,
> God of Abraham, God of Isaac,
>> And God of Jacob;
> Great, mighty and revered God,
>> Highest One,
> Giver of love and goodness,
>> Master of all,
> Who remembers the love of the fathers
>> And brings help to their children's children
> For His name's sake, with love.
>> King, Helper, Savior and Shield.

2.

What can we say about God?

We know about God mostly from traditions found in the Bible. God Himself revealed these things when He spoke to His prophets. Looking in the Bible, we can obtain a very profound concept of God.

Many great thinkers among our sages have written about God. They have delved into all our traditions, analyzing and clarifying them. It is no exaggeration to say that some of the best minds that have ever lived have dealt with the question of God. But for most of them, this was more than a mere intellectual exercise. Their writings were guided by a most deep inspiration and feeling for God. As they thought about God and delved into His mystery, they were also experiencing Him. Thus, our traditions combine both the intellectual and the mystical.

But above all, our traditions go back to the Bible. Almost everything written about God can be found in this Book, if

23

one knows where to look. Searching it carefully, we can build up a picture.

3.

It is clear from all our traditions that we define God primarily as the Creator of all things. We find this in the very opening verse of the Torah, which says, "In the beginning, God created the heaven and the earth." This is a statement about creation, but it also tells us that God is the Creator.[3]

When we speak of God as Creator of "heaven and earth," we are not just speaking of the visible world. God's creation includes every possible thing that exists. The Bible clearly tells us that there is absolutely nothing that is outside the domain of God's creation, as He told His prophet, "I am God, I make all things" (*Isaiah 44:24*).

We may be able to conceive of other universes. There may be worlds beyond our imagination. All of them, however, ultimately emanate from God. This is what the Psalmist meant when he said, "Your dominion is a kingdom of all worlds" (*Psalms 145:13*[4]).

There are many things that are difficult to imagine as emanating from God. For example, there is much evil in the world, and one may be tempted to think of it as coming from a separate power, independent of God. Nothing could be further from the truth; everything ultimately comes from God. If we understand God's purpose in creation, we understand why evil must exist. But it is most important to realize that there is no power independent of God's creation. He therefore told His prophet, "I form light and create darkness, I make peace and create evil, I am God, I do all these things" (*Isaiah 45:7*).

The very word "create"—*Bara* in Hebrew—implies creating something out of nothing. Otherwise, we use the word "make" or "form." When we say that God created the universe, we mean that He created it absolutely *ex nihilo*— out of nothing. This is alluded to in the verse, "He hangs the world upon nothingness" (*Job 26:7*).[5]

The Midrash[6] tells us that a philosopher once remarked to Rabban Gamaliel, "Your God is a wonderful artist, but He had fine materials to work with. When He made the world, He fashioned it out of waste and desolation, darkness, wind, water and the depths."[7] Rabban Gamaliel replied, "Your words are mere wind! All of these things were also created by God."

The act of creation involved absolutely no effort on the part of God. When the Torah says that He "rested" on the seventh day, it does not mean that He rested because He was weary or tired after six days of hard work. Rather, it means that God stopped creating after six days, since the world was completed with the creation of man. The act of creation, however, involved absolutely no effort on the part of God, as the prophet Isaiah taught, "Do you not know? Have you not heard? The Lord, the everlasting God, Creator of the wide world, grows neither weary nor faint" (*Isaiah 40:28*).

This is because God is absolutely infinite. To an infinite Being, the entire universe is like nothing, and therefore, its creation involves no effort. The Bible thus says, "Everything on earth is like nothing to Him, He does as He wills with the host of heaven and the hords of the earth" (*Daniel 4:32*). Every possible thing, even the creation of a universe, is infinitely easy for an infinite God.

In order to emphasize the fact that God's creation involved no effort, the Torah speaks of it as being done with words. Each act of creation begins with the expression "And God said."[8] The Psalmist explicitly states, "With the word of God were the heavens made, with the breath of His mouth, all their host. . . . For He spoke and it was, He commanded, and it stood" (*Psalms 33:6, 9*). The Midrash comments on this: "Not with work nor effort did God create the universe, but with a mere word."[9]

In expressing the absence of effort in the act of creation, our sages teach us that it did not even involve a word, but a mere letter of the alphabet. This furthermore was not just any letter, but the one letter that is most easily pronounced. They teach us that the world was created with the letter *Heh*, the Hebrew equivalent of "H."[10] Pronouncing this letter involves no more effort than the slightest breath. With such a small effort God created the universe.

When we say that the world was created with God's word, we are, of course, using a metaphor. God did not actually speak in a physical sense.[11] He merely willed the existence of all things. His very wisdom and knowledge implied creation. When the Torah says that He spoke, it merely does so to tell us that creation was a willful act. In actuality, however, God's creation came about as a direct result of His wisdom and knowledge.[12] The Prophet said, "He made the earth with His power, founded the world with His wisdom, and unfurled the skies with His understanding" (*Jeremiah 10:12*[13]).

Of course, this also means that creation was an intelligent and purposeful act. God does not act blindly, but with infinite wisdom. We find this concept echoed in the verse, "God founded the earth with wisdom, and fixed the heavens with understanding" (*Proverbs 3:19*).

We therefore see God's work as ultimately perfect. The Torah tells us, "The Creator's work is perfect, for all His ways are just" (*Deuteronomy 32:4*). The Psalmist, too, sings, "God's way is perfect, His word is tried" (Psalms 18:31). We may not be able to see the ultimate perfection in creation, but, in truth, everything has its own perfect time and place. This is the meaning of the verse, "He has made everything perfect in its time" (*Ecclesiastes 3:11*).

Once we say that God is Creator of *everything*, it becomes obvious that there can be no other creator. If there were a second creator, God would have created everything but *it*. The fact that God is Creator of everything therefore implies that He is One and Unique. We hear this in His word to His prophet, "Thus speaks God, Who created the heavens, God, Who formed and made the earth . . . I am God, there is none else" (*Isaiah 45:18*). We shall speak at length of God's unity in a later section.

As Creator of all things, God takes a keen interest in His world, down to the smallest details. The same God Who spins the galaxies also takes care of the hungry child. Nothing in all creation is too trivial for His attention. The Psalmist tells of this in his song, "He made heaven, earth and sea, and all that is in them, He is a true Watcher forever. He provides justice to the oppressed, He gives bread to the hungry" (*Psalms 146:6–7*).

The belief that God is creator of the universe is a foundation of our faith.[14] As discussed earlier, belief in a purposeful Creator is what gives both man and the universe

26

a sense of purpose in existence. The fact that everything was created by one God also provides us with a concept of unity in all creation. It makes every human being a brother under the fatherhood of God. If we are all God's creatures, placed on earth to fulfill His purpose, what possible reason can we have for hatred and warfare? The prophet Malachi expresses this most clearly when he says, "Have we not all one Father? Has not one God created us? Why then do we deal treacherously with one another?" (*Malachi 2:10*).

4.

We can really say very little about God other than that He is the Creator of all things. About God Himself, we can say nothing. We know that He exists, but beyond that, no mind can penetrate.

This is essentially what God told Moses when he asked His name. God replied that His name is, "I Am what I Am." (*Exodus 3:4*). God was saying, "I am. I exist. There is nothing more you can understand about Me."

The only positive thing we can say about God is that He exists. We may experience God, but we cannot understand Him.

Although we cannot comprehend God, we do know Him as Creator, and as such, we understand that certain things must be true about Him. For example, we cannot say that He is any less than any of His creatures. Thus, the very fact that we can see and hear implies that God can do no less. We see this in the words of the Psalmist, "He made the ear, shall He not hear? He formed the eye, shall He not see?" (*Psalms 94:9*).

We therefore say that God at least has every kind of perfection found in the world. Here again, we do not know exactly what this means when speaking of God Himself, but we see His power manifest in creation. All these qualities ultimately come from God, therefore, we cannot say that He Himself does not have them. King David expresses this thought in his prayer, "Yours O God is the greatness, the power, the glory, the victory, the majesty, and everything in heaven and earth. . . . For it is in Your hand to give strength

27

and power to all" (*1 Chronicles 29:11–12*). From the fact that God can grant all these powers, we know that He can also use them.

We must constantly remember that God is the sole Creator of all things. He was the very first, and everything else emanated from Him. It is therefore obvious that God has power over all things. Everything came from Him; therefore, nothing can stop Him or prevent Him from doing as He wishes. God thus told His prophet, "I am God from the beginning of time,[15] none can deliver from my hand. When I act, who can reverse it?" (*Isaiah 43:13*). God is saying that He is the very first and therefore is Creator and Master of all. His power is unlimited, nothing can hold Him back.

We therefore say that God is omnipotent—all powerful. He is the One Creator and Master of all things and there is no power in existence that can turn Him back or frustrate His ultimate purpose. We hear this in the words of Job when he says, "He is in Unity, who can hold Him back? He does what His own will desires" (*Job 23:13*).[16] The same concept is also expressed in Jehoshephat's prayer, "God of our fathers, You alone are God in heaven. You rule over all kingdoms. In Your hand is mighty power, and none can withstand You" (*2 Chronicles 20:5*).

This is one of the important things that we believe about God. He is all powerful and nothing can stand in His way. He rules the world according to His desire. This was one of the very first things that God revealed about Himself when He asked of Abraham, "Is anything too difficult for God?" (*Genesis 18:4*).

God repeats the question to Job, saying, "I am the Lord, God of all flesh. Is anything too difficult for Me?" (*Job 32:27*). He expresses the same thought in the song of Deuteronomy when He says, "I bring both death and life, I wound and I heal. None can deliver from My hand" (*Deuteronomy 32:39*). The same concept is stated in the Prophet's words, "When God decides, who shall cancel it? When He stretches forth His hand, who shall turn it back?" (*Isaiah 14:27*). The Psalmist sums up the idea of God's omnipotence when he sings, "Our God is in heaven, He does whatever He pleases" (*Psalms 115:3*).

God has only to send forth His word and His will is done. As we discussed earlier, this word is not actual speech, but a command that is even more tenuous than thought. When God wills something, it is as good as done. This is what He meant when He told His prophet, "The word that leaves My mouth shall not return to Me unfulfilled. It shall accomplish what I planned, and succeed in what it was sent to do" (*Isaiah 55:10*).

As Creator of the world, God not only is just, but He also defines justice. We cannot think of such concepts as justice and good as independent of God. Even these are His creations, and are therefore defined by Him. To set up an independent standard of justice and good by which to judge God is to place something on the same level as God, and this, of course, we cannot do. God expressed this idea to His prophet when He said, "I have made the world, and man and beast on the face of the earth . . . and I give it to whom I see fit" (*Jeremiah 27:5*). Elihu told Job essentially the same thing, saying, "Who can tell Him what course to take? Who can say, 'You have done wrong'?" (*Job 36:23*).

Since there is no force that can turn God back, there is nothing that can make Him change His mind. Everything in creation fulfills His purpose, and everything that He does leads toward it. No power exists that can change this purpose. This is what God meant when He told His prophet, "I have spoken, I have decided, and I do not repent nor turn back from it" (*Jeremiah 4:28*). It is also what the Torah says, "God is not man that He should lie, nor is He mortal that He should change His mind. Shall He say and not do, or speak and not fulfill it?" (*Numbers 23:19*).

It is for this reason that God is called True. The prophet teaches us, "The Lord, God is Truth. He is the Living God, King of the world" (*Jeremiah 10:10*). Our sages explain this verse by stating: "Why is He true? Because He is the Living God, King of the world. A mortal king may make a promise and not be able to keep it. But God is always able to make His word come true."[17] Our sages similarly teach us that God's seal is Truth.[18]

As Creator, God is Master of all creation. Everything that exists is His and is here to fulfill His purpose. The Torah tells us this, saying, "It all belongs to God: the heaven, the heaven of heaven, the earth, and everything in it" (*Deuteronomy 10:14*). It is also what the prophet means when he says, "This is the plan prepared for the world: It is the Hand stretched over all nations" (*Isaiah 14:26*).

God is the ultimate Ruler over all mankind. Man is given freedom, but ultimately the world's destiny is in God's hands. We are utterly and totally dependent on God, as He Himself told His prophet, "As clay in the potter's hand, so are you in Mine. At one instant, I may decree upon a nation to pluck up, break down and destroy. . . . At another instant, I may decree upon a nation to build up and plant" (*Jeremiah 18:6-9*).

We therefore call God the "King of the universe." This was one of the first things that the Jews realized when they left Egypt, and they exclaimed in the song of the Red Sea, "God is King forever and ever" (*Exodus 15:18*).[19]

We call God a King, but He is like no earthly king. A human monarch may rule, but there are limits to his power. Only God is a King with unlimited ability. The Psalmist thus sings, "God is most high and awesome, a great King over all the world" (*Psalm 47:3*). The prophet Jeremiah sums it all up when he prays, "There is nothing like You, O God. You are great, and Your name is Mighty" (*Jeremiah 10:6*).

5.

As mentioned, there is very little we can say about God Himself. However, we can, to some extent, understand His relationship to His creation.[20]

One of the best analogies of the relationship between God and the world is that of the soul to the body. In a sense, we can call God the "soul" of the universe. Of course, the analogy is far from exact, since God cannot be compared to anything else in creation. But it does serve the useful purpose of clarifying His relationship with the world.

Our sages use the analogy of the soul to the body to explain God's relationship to the world in six basic ways:[21]

> Just as the soul is one in the body,
> so is God one in the universe.
> Just as the soul is pure and above the body,6
> so is God pure and above the world.

30

> Just as the soul does not eat or drink,
>> so God does not eat or drink.
> Just as the soul fills the body,
>> so God fills the world.
> Just as the soul sustains the body,
>> so God sustains the world.
> Just as the soul sees and is unseen,
>> so God sees and is unseen.

These are very basic statements about God. All of them are mentioned many times in our traditions and will be discussed at length. Here we will merely outline them:

1. God is one in the world. He is an absolute unity.

2. God is pure and above the world. He does not partake of any worldly quality. He has neither body, shape nor form. Nothing in all creation can be compared to Him. He is even above such basic worldly concepts as space and time.

3. God does not eat or drink. He is in no way dependent on His creation. Absolutely nothing can be given to God, for ultimately, everything is His.

4. God fills the world. There is no place empty of His presence.

5. God sustains the world. His life-force permeates all creation and gives it existence. If this were removed even for an instant, all creation would instantly cease to exist.

6. God sees and is not seen. He is aware of every single thing in the world, but no creature can see or comprehend God. There is nothing in all creation that can grasp His majesty.

These six concepts provide us with our basic knowledge regarding God's relationship to the world, and we will discuss each one at length. There are a few additional ways in which our sages use this analogy, and we will explore these briefly.

Our sages teach us:

> Just as the soul dwells in the innermost chamber,
>> so God dwells in the innermost chamber.

Here, our sages are teaching us that even though God fills all creation, He does so in a hidden manner. God is everywhere, and yet, no matter how deeply we probe, we cannot detect His presence.[22]

Just as the soul survives the body,
so God survives the world.

This is closely related to the statement that God does not in any way need creation. If the world were to cease to exist, God would still remain the same.

Just as the soul does not sleep,
so God does not sleep.

This alludes to God's constant providence, whereby He is continuously aware of everything in the world and in direct control of all things. There is absolutely no time that His attention is in any way diverted from His creation. This is what the Psalmist meant when he sang, "The Guardian of Israel does not doze nor sleep" (*Psalms 121:4*). God's providence is constant and continuous.

6.

One of the most important foundations of our faith is the belief that God is one.[23]

The Torah says, "Hear O Israel, the Lord is our God, the Lord is One" (*Deuteronomy 6:4*).

This is the *Sh'ma*, our declaration of faith. Twice each day, the believing Jew cries out these words. They are among the first things a Jew learns as a child, and the last words that he utters before he dies. On every Jewish doorpost, there is a Mezuzah proclaiming these very same words. They are found again in the Tefillin, bound daily next to the heart and mind. All these proclaim this most basic principal of Judaism.

What this tells us is that all things come from One ultimate Source. All creation is bound together by God. There is One unifying Force in the universe, God alone, unique and incomparable. The Torah thus tells us, "Know it this day, and set it in your heart, that the Lord is God, in heaven above, and on the earth below, there is no other" (*Deuteronomy 4:39*).

As Creator of all things, God stands alone. There can be only one Creator of all things. The Psalmist thus sings, "Who besides the Lord is God? Who besides our God is Creator?" (*Psalms 18:32*).

There can only be one First Thing. Anything else is no longer first. God alone is the First Thing, as He told His prophet, "I am first and I am last, and beside Me there is no God. . . . There is no other God besides Me, no other Creator. This I know" (*Isaiah 44:6, 8*).

Man must ultimately depend on God. All of our prayers are directed toward Him. God is the One who has all power, and all our hopes and aspirations depend on Him. God thus told us through His prophet, "Before Me, there was no God, and none shall be after Me. I Myself am God, and none but I can save you" (*Isaiah 43:10,11*).

For over a thousand years the Jews alone proclaimed that God was One. For the first thousand years of our existence, the rest of the world believed in a host of pagan gods, each with a different power. Even those who believed in God felt that He was too high to be concerned with man, and therefore acted only through mediators. These mediators then became their gods.[24] Others believed that there were two primary forces, one for good and the other for evil.[25] Alone of all peoples, the Jew believed that everything ultimately and directly emanated from one Source, namely, God. Our experience at the Exodus, reinforced throughout our history, also taught us that God Himself is concerned with man, and to Him alone we must pray. God spoke of this when He told us through His prophet, "I am the Lord your God since your days in Egypt. You know that there is no God but Me, and no one else can save you" (*Hosea 13:4*).

We see the processes of history gradually bringing the entire world to belief in one God. The pagan world gradually gave way to religions professing belief in the one God of Israel. More and more, people are becoming convinced of this truth and in the end, the entire world will believe. The Prophet thus proclaimed, "God shall be King over all the world, and on that day, God will be One, and His name One" (*Zechariah 14:9*).

7.

Just as God is One, so is He unique. There is absolutely no power that can compare to Him. He is the One from whom all power emanates. This was one of the first things the Jewish people understood about God after the Exodus, and they sang by the Red Sea, "Who is like You, O God, among the mighty? Who is like You, majestic in holiness, awesome in praise, working wonders?" (*Exodus 15:11*).

Nothing else can possibly resemble God. He is the Creator of all things, and as such, is unique. Hannah thus said in her prayer, "There is none holy like God, for there is none besides Him. There is no Creator like our God" (*1 Samuel 2:2*). God Himself told His prophet, "To whom will you liken Me, or make Me equal, or compare Me that we may be alike? . . . I am God, and there is none else. I am God, and there is none like Me" (*Isaiah 46:5,9*).

As Creator, God stands unique. Other beings may be great and powerful, but they can never be the one Creator of all. No matter what, this difference must exist.[26] God may have created many lofty beings, but none can even come close to resembling Him. The Psalmist thus sang (*Psalms 89:7*):

Who in the skies can compare to God?
    Who is like Him of the sons of might?
A God too dreadful for the holy ones,
    Too great and awesome for all around Him.
O Lord of Hosts, who is like You?
    Mighty God, girded with faith.

8.

One of the foundations of our faith is the belief that God does not have any body, shape or form. After the revelation at Sinai, God specifically warned us, "Consider this carefully: You saw no manner of form on the day that God spoke to you at Horeb (Sinai)" (*Deuteronomy 4:15*).[27]

The fact that God has no body or form should be perfectly obvious. If God had any shape, it would provide us with a means of comparison. Since we have already determined that

34

He cannot be compared to anything, it is clear that He has no body or form.

This also follows from the fact that God is infinite. God cannot have a body, because anything with a body must be bounded and finite. The Prophet sums up this line of reasoning when he says, "All the nations are like nothing before Him. They are like zero and nothingness to Him. To whom then will you liken God? What likeness will you compare to Him?" (*Isaiah 40:17,18*).[28]

The very fact that there is nothing in our experience that compares to God makes it utterly impossible really to speak of Him. Our vocabulary, and indeed, our very thought processes, can only deal with things we know. Since God can in no way be compared to anything in our experience, we do not even have the vocabulary with which to speak about Him.[29]

Our sages teach us that God borrows terms from His creatures to express His relationship with the world.[30] God can only speak to us in language that we understand. We therefore have a rule: "The Torah speaks in the language of man."[31]

We normally address God as we would address another person. It is therefore natural for the Torah to do so. Thus, when the Torah describes God's action, it may speak of God's hand. When it says that He sees us, it may speak of His eye. In saying that we are lower than He, it may say that we are under His feet.[32] None of these expressions, however, is meant to imply that God has any body or form. They are merely spoken in allegory, relating to His power and action in the world.[33]

Although these anthropomorphisms are spoken in allegory, they do have a precise meaning. They speak of the various qualities that God uses in running His universe, and as such, are the basic ingredients of His providence. We find a hint of their meaning in Elijah's introduction in the *Tikuney Zohar*, where he says:[34]

> Love is the right hand,
>   Power is the left;
> Glory is the body,
>   Victory and Splendor are the two feet . . .

> Wisdom is the brain,
>> Understanding is the heart . . .
>> Majesty is the mouth . . .

All these spiritual qualities also exist in man. The Torah therefore says, "God created man in His image" (*Genesis 1:27*). We are not speaking of physical form, but of spiritual quality. As we mentioned earlier, God can to some extent be thought of as the soul of the world. As such, His spiritual qualities may parallel those of the human soul. In a spiritual sense, then, man is created in the "image of God."[35] Furthermore, since man's body parallels his soul, it too partakes of the divine.[36]

Every time God uses an anthropomorphism to describe Himself, He does so to teach us a lesson. There is a Midrash that expresses this most lucidly:[37]

> When our fathers stood at Mount Sinai to receive the Torah, they did not see any form. They did not see the form of any man, any creature, or even of any soul that God created in His world. It is thus written, "Consider this carefully: You saw no manner of form on the day that God spoke to you at Horeb."
>
> You want to argue that God is fire. . . . You ask, is it not written, "God is a consuming fire" (*Deuteronomy 4:24*)?
>
> Let me give you an example:
>
> A king once had a family and servants who did not act correctly. He said to them, "I am a bear upon you! I am a lion upon you! I am the angel of death upon you! All because of your deeds!"
>
> When the Torah says, "God is a consuming fire," we must interpret it the same way. . . . Thus, it is also written, "God will judge with fire . . . " (*Isaiah 66:16*).

9.

When we say that God is pure and holy, we mean that He is totally separated from anything worldly. In general, the word "holy" means different, separated, special and set aside.[38] When we apply it to God, it means that He does not partake of any worldly quality. There is nothing in the world that can give us even the slightest clue of God's true essence. We find an allusion to this in the verse, " 'To whom will you liken Me that I be an equal?' says the Holy One" (*Isaiah 40:25*). In this verse we see that God is called the "Holy One" precisely because He cannot be likened to anything in His creation.

What do we mean when we say that God is totally divorced from all worldly things?

First of all, we mean that He is not physical in any sense, and therefore, not made of matter. This should be obvious, since God is the Creator of all matter. We mean that God has no body, shape or form, as we have already discussed. If we look into this a bit more deeply, however, we understand that as soon as we say that God has no body or form, we are also saying that it is utterly impossible to imagine Him. We have absolutely no way of picturing something without form, and therefore, have no way of imagining God. When we say that God does not partake of wnything worldly, we are also saying that He is utterly beyond our imagination.

There are other worldly things that are even more basic than matter and form. There are things like space and time, which are the most elementary ingredients of the physical world. It is utterly impossible even to begin to imagine a world without space. It is like trying to look through the back of your head. And to imagine a universe without time is even more hopeless. We cannot even see two times at once. The absence of time is utterly beyond our ability to comprehend.

One of the ways in which God is holy is in the fact that He exists in a realm where neither space nor time exist. The Prophet says of God, "He dwells in eternity on high, His name is holy" (*Isaiah 57:15*). Eternity is where neither space nor time exist. God is in this unimaginable domain, and is therefore called "holy."

To try to speak or philosophize about the realm of God is utterly impossible. Our minds cannot even begin to operate in a realm where neither space or time exist. We do not have the vocabulary to express the elements of such a domain. This is but one reason why God is absolutely beyond our understanding.[39]

All this is well expressed by an anecdote recorded in the Midrash: [40]

A philosopher once asked Rabban Gamaliel, "Where is God?"

The Rabbi answered, "I do not know."

The philosopher retorted, "He is your praise and wisdom. You pray to Him every day. How can you say that you do not know where He is?"

Rabban Gamaliel looked at the philosopher and said, "You are asking me about something that is very far off, way beyond our world. I will ask you about something that is very close to you. Where is your soul?"

The philosopher was puzzled. He replied, "I really do not know."

Rabbi Gamaliel said, "Then your words are mere wind. You do not even know the place of something that is actually a part of you. How can you question me about something that is beyond understanding?"

What Rabban Gamaliel was telling the philosopher is that there are some things that the mind cannot even begin to grasp. To ask questions about these things is not wisdom, but foolishness. To ask where God is, is like asking where is thought or love or goodness. There are things outside the physical domain, and to apply physical terms to them is to lose sight of their true meaning.

The Midrash also tells us that even the highest angels cannot comprehend God's place. They therefore merely praise God by singing, "Blessed is God's glory from His place" (*Ezekiel 3:12*).[41] Even these celestial creatures, who themselves live in a realm beyond physical space, still cannot comprehend the domain of God. It is holy—utterly unique and different than anything in all creation.

When we say that God is the Creator of all things, we must say that He is the Creator of space and time as well.[42] Before He created the world, He created a realm of space and time in which to place it.[43] Thus, it is God Who defines space and time, and we cannot say that He is defined by them.

There is another Midrash that throws light on this most obscure subject.[44] The Midrash notes that in many places, God is called *Makom*, which literally means "place." The Midrash asks, "Why is God called 'Place'?" It answers, "Because He is the Place of the world. The world is not His place."

The Midrash is not merely telling us that God is bigger than the universe and therefore contains it inside of Himself. It is speaking in a much deeper sense. It is God Who defines the very concept of "place." He is Creator of space and time, and as such, is what makes them exist. As Creator of the concept of "place," God is the Place of all creation.

The Midrash finds an allusion to this in a verse in the Torah that literally reads, "Behold, 'place' is with Me" (*Exodus 33:21*).[45] "Place" is something that is *with* God, defined by Him. An even more remarkable allusion is found by the Midrash[46] in the Psalm (*Psalms 90:1,2*):

> God, You have been our abode for all generations,
> Before the mountains were born,
> Before the world was formed,
> From eternity to eternity, You are God.

What the Psalm is saying is that God Himself dwells in Eternity, and as such, is the "abode" of all creation. God is "from eternity to eternity," beyond the realm of space and time. It is therefore He who creates space and time as an "abode" for His creation.

According to many thinkers, space and time are properties of matter.[47] Therefore, when God created a universe of matter, He also created space and time.

Although the Bible does not discuss it in philosophical terms, there are numerous allusions to the fact that God is Creator and Master of time and space. Thus, for example, the Psalmist sings, "Yours is the day, Yours is also the night . . . You have set the borders of the world, You have made summer and winter" (*Psalms 74:16,17*). The Psalmist alludes again to the creation of space when he says to God, "You created north and south" (*Ibid. 89:13*). Direction is the most elementary ingredient of space, and here we see that it, too, is created by God. In utter nothingness there is neither space nor direction. The first act of creation is therefore the creation of space out of nothingness. Job alludes to this most remarkably when he says, "He stretches the north over nothingness" (*Job 26:7*).[48] Another allusion is found in God's word to His prophet, which states, "I am He, I am the first, I am also the last. My hand laid the foundation of the world, My right hand spread out the heavens. When I call to them, they stand together" (*Isaiah 48:12*).

Since God encompasses all space and time, we see Him as infinite in them. Just as God's kingdom extends to all worlds, so is it infinite in time. The Psalmist thus says, "Your

generations" (*Psalms 145:13*).

The concept of God's eternity is repeated over and over in the Bible. In the Song of the Red Sea, our fathers sang, "God shall be King forever and ever" (*Exodus 15:18*). The Psalmist echoes these words when he says, "God is King forever" (*Psalms 9:8*).[49] Even in our darkest hour, we did not forget this lesson, as we chant in our dirge, "You, O God, sit forever, Your throne endures from generation to generation" (*Lamentations 5:19*).

God exists outside of time, and therefore, we cannot apply any concepts involving time to Him. Thus, we cannot say that God has a beginning or end, or that the concept of age applies to Him in any way. In one place, the Talmud flatly asks, "How can we possibly say that God grows old?"[50]

All change takes place in time. When something changes, it is in one state at one moment, and in another at the next. Since God exists outside of time, it is impossible for Him to change. God thus told His prophet, "I am God, I do not change" (*Malachi 3:6*). The Psalmist, also, sang, "You are the same, Your years never end" (*Psalms 102:28*).

God is therefore the unmoved Mover. He can bring about change in His world without changing Himself. He is the creator of time, and as such, can do whatever He desires with it. Thus, it is not incomprehensible that He can cause change without being changed Himself.[51]

Even the creation of the universe did not change God in any way. He did not suddenly make up His mind to create a world. The plan of creation existed in timeless eternity, and was only brought into time when time itself was created.[52] God, however, remains exactly the same after as before creation.[53]

This is expressed most clearly in our prayer *Adon Olom*:

> Lord of the world, Who was King
> Before all forms were created;
> When all things were made by His will,
> Only then was His name called King.

What this song is saying is that God was the same King before creation as He was after it. The only difference is that now He is *called* King. Before creation, there was nothing to call Him King.

These concepts are most difficult to understand. As we have repeated several times, it is actually impossible to imagine a realm where neither change nor time exist. We are glancing through a crack in the door, but the human mind can never really enter into it, at least not in this life.

In many places in the Torah, we find accounts of God expressing such emotions as joy or anger. At first glance, these may seem to imply changes in God's emotions. But further thought should remind us of our previous discussion of human terms when used in relationship to God. Here again, we are merely perceiving God's acts, and ascribing the same emotions to Him as we ourselves would feel if we were doing the same thing. Thus, for example, when God does something to punish, we say that He is angry. When He bountifully rewards, we say that He is happy. In all these cases, however, we are merely expressing how we would feel if we were doing these things. It is most important to realize that they do not imply any change in God Himself.[54]

God literally never changes His mind, and therefore, His truth is absolute. A human being can say something in all sincerity one day, but feel quite differently the next. This is not true of God. He never changes; and that which is true in His realm today is also true tomorrow. God is therefore the only absolute truth.

The Prophet thus says, "The Lord, God, is Truth" (*Jeremiah 10:10*). The Midrash gives the following explanation:[55]

> What is God's seal? Our Rabbi said in the name of Rabbi Reuven, "God's seal is Truth."[56]
>
> Resh Lakish asked, "Why is *Emeth* the Hebrew word for truth?"
>
> He replied, "Because it is spelled *Aleph Mem Tav*. *Aleph* is the first letter of the Hebrew alphabet, *Mem* is the middle letter, and *Tav* is the last letter of the alphabet. God thus says, 'I am first and I am last.' "

The Midrash is making precisely this point. In saying that God is Truth, we are also saying that He is eternal. Truth is

41

something that is absolute and does not change. When we say that God is Truth, we are saying the He is outside the realm of change.[57]

The final consequence of God's eternity is the fact that He knows the future. Since He is outside of time, future and past are exactly the same to Him, and His knowledge of the future is therefore exactly the same as His knowledge of the past. This will be discussed at length in the section on God's omniscience, but it also concerns our present discussion. God knows the future because He exists outside of time, as He Himself told His prophet, "I call the generations from the beginning, I, God, am First, and with the last, I am the same" (*Isaiah 41:4*). The prophet is alluding to the reason why God can know the future and "call the generations from the beginning." This is because He is outside of time, abiding in unchanging Eternity from the beginning to the end.[58]

As Creator of both, God sees space and time alike. He can look at time just like we look at space. We are constantly moving through time, and can therefore only see the present. We are like a person driving down a road, who only sees a small part of the road at any given time. A person in an airplane, however, can see the entire road at once. In a similar way, God sees all time, from the beginning to the end, all at once. This is what the Talmud means when it says, "He sees it all with a single glance."[59]

10.

When our sages teach us that God does not eat or drink, they are telling us that He derives nothing at all from the world. God is the Creator and Giver, and there is no one who can give Him anything. God thus speaks through the Psalmist and says, "Even if I were hungry, I would not tell you, for the earth and everything in it are Mine" (*Psalms 50:12*). The Midrash tells us that God is saying, "Can you give oil to the olive or wine to the grape? If not, how can you give anything to Me?"[60]

God is saying that the olive and the grape are the givers of oil and wine; therefore, one cannot give these products to them. Furthermore, even these are creations of God. God is

42

the Giver of everything; and therefore, one certainly cannot give anything to Him.

There is a story in the Talmud (*Chulin 61a*) that illustrates this point quite clearly:

A king once said to Rabbi Joshua, "I would like to prepare a meal for your God."

Rabbi Joshua told the king that this could not be done, assuring him that God has no need for this, having many servants to provide for Him. When the king insisted, the Rabbi advised him to prepare a meal on a large open space on the bank of the Ravisa River. The king assembled a large army, and they worked all summer, gathering grain for this "meal." Before they were able to finish their preparation, however, a strong wind came and blew it all into the river. They worked again all that autumn, amassing a huge mountain of grain for the "meal." But again a torrential rain came, washing it all into the river.

The king asked Rabbi Joshua, "Who is taking away your God's meal?"

The Rabbi replied, "These are merely His janitors, who sweep and mop before Him."

The king then agreed that nothing could be given to God.

What this story is telling us is that God's power is infinite. Even if He had any needs, He could supply them Himself. However, no such needs exist in the first place.

God has absolutely no need for the world. We cannot even say that creation filled some inner need for God.[61] Creation was an act of pure love and altruism, with God gaining absolutely nothing from it at all. Nothing can change God, and even though He is the Creator of the world, He can exist exactly the same without it.[62] The Psalmist speaks of this when he sings (*Psalms 102:26–28*):

> Long ago, You founded the earth,
> The heavens are the work of Your hands.
> They will perish, but You will remain. . . .
> You are the same, Your years have no end.

One might be tempted to think that God may have created the world out of curiosity, to see how it would turn out. But even this is not true. We have already discussed how God knows the future exactly as He knows the past and present. He did not gain any new knowledge with the creation of the world or with anything else that happens in it. It is God who defines knowledge, and nothing can impart new knowledge to Him. This is what Job meant when he asked, "Can anyone grant God knowledge, when He judges even the highest?" (*Job 21:22*). The highest reaches of wisdom and knowledge are judged and defined by God. Who can add anything to His knowledge?

The Prophet echoes this question when he says (*Isaiah 40:13-14*):

> Who can affect God's spirit?
> What counselor can instruct Him?
> Whom has He consulted for understanding?
> Who taught Him the way of justice?
> Or gave Him lessons in wisdom?

Our good deeds do not affect God or benefit Him in any way. Our sins do not do anything to harm Him. All morality and good were created only for our own benefit.[63] Our sages thus taught us, "The commandments were only given to purify His creatures."[64] God Himself is not affected by any of them, as Elihu told Job (*Job 35:6-8*),

> If you sin, how does it touch Him?
> If you do much evil, how can you harm Him?
> If you do good, what do you give Him?
> What does he gain from your deeds?
> Your evil is only against man,
> And your good is only for mortals.

Our sages teach us that all the good that man does only benefits the man who does it, even in religious acts directed toward God.[65] Although God wants our service, He in no way needs it.

God Himself sums this up in His theophany to Job when He says, "Who has given Me anything beforehand that I should repay him? Everything under heaven is Mine" (*Job 41:3*). God does not reward good because it benefits Him, but because it is good. No one can give God anything at all, even good deeds. Our sages comment on this passage and tell us that God is saying, "Who can hang a Mezuzah if I do not give him a house? Who can build a Succah if I do not give him place?"[66] We cannot do anything unless God gives us the means. Therefore, everything that we do is ultimately done with things that belong to God. Indeed, our very existence belongs to God. This being the case, what can we give Him?[67]

God is the Giver of all things. As such, there is nothing that He can receive from His creation.

11.

From all this, we might begin to think of God as being very remote, beyond the realm of human experience. We might be led to believe that God is far away, disinterested in human suffering and indifferent to our prayers. But the exact opposite is true. God may transcend the very fabric of space and time. He might be absolutely unimaginable. But still, He is very close.

Our understanding of God is twofold. We see Him as both imminent and transcendental. He both encompasses and fills all creation.[68] This is what the Psalmist means when he sings, (*Psalm 113:5,6*)

> Who is like the Lord our God
>> Who is enthroned on high,
> Yet looks down low
>> Upon both heaven and earth.

Of course, this apparent duality exists only because of our imperfect understanding of God. He Himself is an absolute unity.[69]

We look at God in both of these ways. We see God as a King, sitting remotely on an exalted throne, far above the reaches of our imagination. But we also see Him as our heavenly Father, close at hand and ready to listen to our troubles and share our problems.

One of our well-known prayers addresses God as *Avinu Malkenu*—"our Father, our King." First we approach God as our Father, who is close and relates to our needs. Only then do we remind ourselves that He is also our King, remote, transcendental, heavenly and exalted.

We find this same idea in every blessing we make. We begin each blessing with the words, "Blessed are You, O

Lord, our God, King of the universe." In every blessing we must recognize God's majesty, [70] calling Him King and Master of the world. But before we call God King of the world, we insert another idea. We call Him "our God." Before we proclaim that God is the transcendental King of the universe, we recall that He is also *our* God. He is ours to speak to, to pray to and to bare our hearts to.

Whenever we speak of God, we state that He is first and foremost *our* God. Only after we remind ourselves of this do we proclaim that He is King of the universe.

We find the same concept in the *Sh'ma,* our declaration of faith, where we declare "Hear O Israel, the Lord is our God, the Lord is One" (*Deuteronomy 6:4*). [71] When we say that God is One, we are proclaiming one of the deepest of all mysteries. We say that God is One—over all the stars and galaxies of the universe. God is One with an awesome unity that is beyond all human comprehension. Before we proclaim this great truth, we pause to reflect on another equally important truth: "The Lord is *our* God." He is ours, and listens to our prayers when we call upon Him. God may exist in majestic Unity, but He is also ours to call upon.

Our sages teach us that He is our God in this world, but One in the next. In the future world, God will open our minds so that we will be able to comprehend the mystery of His unity. But here in this world He is our God, and we know Him only by the way we ourselves can relate to Him. [72]

This concept is expressed most vividly in the *Kedushah,* the song of the angels. As we have seen, one part of their song is "Blessed is God's glory from His place" (*Ezekiel 3:12*). The angels are praising a transcendental God, far above the comprehension of even the highest beings. They are chanting of God's glory in a place beyond, far above all creation.

But there is another part of their song preceding this. The angels also sing "Holy, holy, holy, is the Lord of Hosts, all the world is filled with His glory" (*Isaiah 6:3*). Here they are singing to an imminent God, who is near and fills all the world. God may be far above our minds, further than the stars and the infinite places beyond the stars. And yet, He is also very close to us. We therefore say in the Sabbath *Kedushah* prayer, "His glory fills the world, His servants ask one another, 'Where is the place of His glory?' "

46

Our sages teach us that "just as the soul fills the body, so God fills the world." There is absolutely no place empty of God. [73] God's essence permeates every atom of our being and every spark of our soul. His power extends to the very essence of every element of creation.

God's omnipresence is most beautifully expressed by the Psalmist, who sings(*Psalms 139:7–12*):

> Where can I go from Your spirit?
> > Where can I flee from Your presence?
> If I climb the heavens, You are there,
> > If I plumb the depths, You are there.
> If I flew to the point of sunrise,
> > Or dwelt at the limit of the sea,
> Your hand would still guide me,
> > Your right hand would hold me.
> If I asked darkness to cover me,
> > The black of night to hide me,
> The darkness is not dark to You
> > The night is as bright as day,
> > Both light and darkness are the same.

There is no place in all creation where one can in any way escape God's presence. From the highest heaven to the lowest pit, He permeates all things. God Himself expressed this to His prophet when He said "If they dig down to the bowels of the earth, My hand will haul them out. If they scale the heavens, My hands will drag them down" (*Amos 9:2*).

This concept is illuminated by a Midrashic anecdote. [74] A Roman once asked Rabban Gamaliel, "Why did God appear to Moses in a lowly bush?"

The Rabbi replied, "If God had appeared in a carob or fig tree, you would have asked the same question. God appeared in a lowly bush to teach us that He fills all creation. He could speak to Moses even from the most lowly thornbush."

Rabbi Pinchas sheds even more light on this concept in another Midrash. [75] He says, "When a mortal king is in his bedroom, he is not in his throne room. When he is in his throne room, he is not in his bedroom. But the Holy One fills the highest and the lowest. It is thus written 'His glory is in heaven and in earth' (*Psalms 148:13*)."

Since God fills all creation, He is close when we call Him. The Psalmist thus sings "God is near to all who call Him, to all who call Him in truth" (*Psalms 145:18*). We do not have to seek in far places or indulge in deep philosophical speculation to find God. All we need do is call upon Him with sincerity and truth.

We also experience God's closeness when we obey His commandments. Keeping the commandments is the main way in which we approach God.[76] This is what the Torah means when it says "Love the Lord your God, obey His word, so that you may hold fast to Him" (*Deuteronomy 30:22*). The Psalmist is also expressing this when he sings, "You are close, O God, for all Your commandments are truth" (*Psalms 119:151*).

Although God fills all creation, there are times when we see and feel His presence more than others. There are places where God tells us that His presence is to be found. For example, we are taught that the Divine Presence is in every congregation of worship, as it is written, "God stands in the Godly congregation" (*Psalms 82:1*).[77]

The idea is expanded in the following Talmudic anecdote:[78]

A nonbeliever once said to Rabban Gamaliel, "You say that God is in every congregation of ten. But there are many such congregations. How many can God be?"

Rabban Gamaliel asked him if the sun was shining where they were now standing. When the other replied that it was, the Rabbi asked him, "Then is the sun also shining over your house?"

The nonbeliever replied, "Of course it is. The sun shines over all the earth."

Rabban Gamaliel replied, "The sun is only one of God's multitude of servants. If it can shine over the entire world, God's glory certainly can."

God Himself told those who sought Him that He would always be close to them. Thus, He told Jacob, "I am with you, and will keep you wherever you go" (*Genesis 28:15*). This closeness to God is perhaps best expressed in the most famous of psalms, where the Psalmist sings out(*Psalm 23*):

> God is my Shepherd,
> I have no wants;
> He lets me lie in green pastures
> He leads me to still waters,

He restores my soul.
He guides me in straight paths
For the sake of His name.
Though I pass through the valley
Of the shadow of death
I will fear no evil
For You are with me.
Your rod and Your staff,
They comfort me.

When the Torah says that God is in a place, it is not really saying anything about God. God is in every place, and cannot be restricted to any one locality. When we say that God is in a place, we are really saying something about that place. We are saying that it is a place where God's presence is felt, or where His miracles are seen.[79] The *Mekhilta*, the most ancient Midrash on the Book of Exodus, expresses this very clearly:[80]

It is written, "And God went before them by day in a pillar of cloud . . . and by night in a pillar of fire" (*Exodus 13:21*). But how is it possible to say this? Is it not written, "The whole earth is filled with His glory"? (*Isaiah 6:3*).

Rabbi Antoninos explained this with the following example:

A king once sat in judgment and remained in court until after dark. His children remained in court so that they would be able to accompany him home.

When the king left for his palace, he took a lantern and carried it, lighting the way for his children. His officers and nobles saw this and offered to carry the lantern for the king.

The king then told them, "I do not carry the lamp because I lack someone else to carry it. I carry it to show my love for my children."

Rabbi Antoninos explained that the same is true of God. He reveals His glory before His children as an expression of love for them.

The Talmud takes this idea one step further and teaches us a general lesson: "It is not the place that gives honor to the man. It is the man who gives honor to the place." It then derives this lesson from God Himself. As long as God's presence was on Mount Sinai, no one was allowed to climb it. As long as His glory was in the tabernacle, no unclean man could approach it. But when His glory left these places, any one could enter. [81]

What the Talmud is teaching us is that God may say that His glory is in a certain place, but that does not mean that it is not elsewhere. When God tells us that His glory is in a given location, He is saying that He is the One "who gives honor to the place." Hillel thus said in God's name, "When I am here, everything is here. When I am not here, nothing is here." [82]

God's glory fills all creation, but it can only be felt where man prepares the way. It is not enough to say that we believe that God fills all creation. We must do something about it. We must act as if we realize that He is everywhere. The Talmud teaches us that a person who sins in a hidden place is pushing away the feet of the Divine Presence. [83]

We cannot come close to God by building beautiful synagogues and temples. The only way is by being humble and obeying God's word. God Himself told us this through His prophet (*Isaiah 66:1,2*):

> The heavens are My throne,
>   The earth is My footstool,
> Where will you build a house for Me?
>   Where shall My resting place be?
> Everything was made by My hand,
>   And all this is Mine . . .
> But My eyes are drawn to the man
>   Of humble and contrite spirit
>   Who trembles at My word.

There is an anecdote that sums this up. It is told that the famed Chassidic leader, Rabbi Menachem Mendel of Kotzk, once asked his disciples, "Where does God live?" They quickly answered, "God lives everywhere." But the Rabbi would not accept their answer. He taught them, "God lives wherever man lets Him in."

One of the reasons why we cannot see God is because He is so very close to us. We cannot see Him for the very same reason that we cannot see the atmosphere. We live, breathe and move in an ocean of air, and yet it remains invisible to us. We understand that the atmosphere is invisible because of its very nature and closeness to us.

God is invisible for much the same reason. The reason we cannot see Him is not so much because He is so far away, as because He is so near to us. He fills all creation and there is no place empty of Him; therefore, we have no comparison with which to detect His presence. Of course there are deeper reasons, but they are beyond the scope of this work.

The only time we are aware of the air around us is when we feel it, such as when the wind blows. Similarly, the only time we are aware of God is when He acts to reveal His presence. This may be the reason why the Hebrew language has the same word, *Ruach,* for both wind and spirit.

We can feel God's presence if we only let Him in. It may be during the synagogue prayers, or while singing the Sabbath *zemiroth.* It may be while dancing on Simchath Torah, or while binding oneself with Tefillin. Or it might be when one just steals away to be alone with God, deep in the woods, on a lonely mountain peak, or standing in a field, gazing at the passing clouds and wondering at the meaning of it all. Who has not looked up at the heavens on a clear bright night and stared with fixed attention, as if he could penetrate the fathomless depths of space and probe the hearts of the stars and steal their secret?

This may indeed have been the experience of the Psalmist. It might have been a clear night, and as he gazed up at the heavens, he compared their glory to his own small self. Gazing at a myriad of stars, he burst into song (*Psalm 8:4-6*):

When I look at Your heavens,
     The work of Your fingers,
The moon and the stars
     That You have established;
What is man that You think of him?
     Mere mortal that You remember him?
But You have made him a little less than God,
     You crowned him with glory and honor.

There are times when we feel that God is there, right next to us. At times like these we can realize just how close God really is. Our whole being, body and soul, can be swallowed up in the Absolute Being that is God. We become steeped and saturated with God, and feel Him closer to us than existence itself.

12.

Our sages teach us, "Just as the soul sustains the body, so God sustains the world." As discussed earlier, this means that God's life-force permeates all creation and constantly gives it existence. Thus, existence itself is a direct result of God's constant power. This is the meaning of the song of the Levites, who chanted to God "You made the heavens, the heavens of heaven . . . the earth and everything in it . . . and You give life to all" (Nehemiah 9:6). God constantly gives life and existence to all creation.

Our sages interpret this verse and teach us, "Do not read MeChayeh—gives life—but MeHaveh—gives existence." [84] The verse would then read, "You give existence to all." The power that God gives His creation is more than mere life. It is existence itself. Daniel therefore calls God "The Life of the world" (Daniel 12:7). [85]

A human craftsman can build a house and then forget it. But God's creation is more than that. Not only was God's will responsible for creation, it is also responsible for the continued existence of all things. Nothing can exist without God willing it to exist. If He did not constantly will the existence of everything in creation, it would utterly cease to exist. [86] Elihu thus told Job "If He would gather to Himself His spirit and breath, then all flesh would perish together" (Job 34:14,15). [87] The Psalmist, too, sang "You hide Your face, they vanish; You withdraw their spirit, they perish" (Psalms 104:29).

In our daily morning prayer, we say, "In His goodness, He constantly renews the act of creation. Thus it is written "He *makes* great lights, for His love is infinite" (Psalms 136:7). The prayer quotes this verse, stressing that the word "makes" is used, in the present tense, rather than "made" in the past. God did not just make the world. He constantly "makes" it, continually renewing the act of creation.

The Midrash [88] teaches us that the very same word with which God created the universe constantly sustains its existence. This is based upon the following Psalm (Psalms 119:89–91):

Eternal is Your word, O God,
Planted firm in the heavens,

52

Your faithfulness lasts for all ages,
You founded the earth and it stands.
Creation is maintained by Your ruling,
For all things are Your servants.

13.

The belief that God knows all the deeds of man is one of the foundations of our faith. [89]

As discussed earlier, God's being both fills and constantly sustains all creation. The very fact that God's presence is everywhere allows Him to be continuously aware of everything that takes place in His creation. God gives existence to everything, and there is no place to hide from Him. This is what He Himself told His prophet, "I am a God near at hand . . . not a God far off. Can a man hide himself in secret places that I not see him? . . . Do I not fill heaven and earth?" (Jeremiah 22:23,24).

As mentioned earlier, our sages teach us, "Just as the soul sees and is not seen, so God sees and is not seen." Our sages are telling us that the fact that God sees and the fact that He is not seen are related. Both stem from the fact that He is so near and permeates all creation. As discussed earlier, this is one of the main reasons why we cannot see Him. It is also the reason why He sees all.

There is no place in all creation that escapes God's scrutiny. He perceives everything that happens in the world, never lifting His gaze from it. The wise Solomon thus said "God's eyes are in every place, keeping watch on the evil and the good" (Proverbs 15:3). Job was also expressing this when he said "He looks to the ends of the earth, and sees under the whole heaven" (Job 28:24).

There is no place where one can hide from God. Light and darkness are absolutely the same to Him. Nothing in all creation can be hidden from Him. Here again we find the words of Job, "He uncovers deep things out of darkness, and brings the deep gloom to light" (Job 12:22). He repeats the same theme when he exclaims "He brings hidden things forth to light" (Ibid. 28:11).

God is constantly aware of every single human being, and indeed, of everything in all creation. This is what Solomon meant when he said "The ways of man are before God's eyes" (*Proverbs 5:21*). Elihu also expressed this concept to Job, saying "His eyes keep watch over all man's ways. He observes their every step. There is no darkness nor deep shadow where the sinner can hide" (*Job 34:21*). God Himself told this to His prophet, declaring "My eyes are upon all their ways, they are not hidden from My face. Their sin is never concealed from My eyes" (*Jeremiah 16:17*).

The Psalmist was completely aware that God was always watching him. It was he who set God continuously before him. He cried out "O God, You know my folly, my sins are not hidden from You" (*Psalm 69:6*). In a Psalm quoted earlier, he sings of this (*Psalm 139:1-6*):

O God, You examine me and know me:
You know when I sit and stand,
    You read my thoughts from far off.
When I walk or lie down, You are watching,
    You know well all of my ways.
The word is not yet on my tongue,
    Before You, O God, know about it . . .
Such knowledge is beyond my grasp,
    A height my mind cannot reach.

There is no secret before God and no hiding place in all creation where things can be concealed from Him. The deepest recesses of man's heart are wide open before Him. Daniel thus tells us "He uncovers deep secrets. He knows what lies in darkness, the light dwells with Him" (*Daniel 2:22*).

The Midrash explains this with a parable.[90] A master architect was appointed as tax collector. Once, he was sent to a city that he himself had built. When he designed this city, he built into it many underground passages and secret chambers.

Upon hearing that a new tax collector was coming, the citizens hid their money in these secret chambers, thinking that he would not be able to find them. When the architect-tax collector got wind of this, he told the people, "I myself built these hiding places. Do you think you can hide things from me in them?"

The Midrash explains that God is like this architect. He tells us, "I created you and formed the innermost recesses of your hearts. What can you possibly hide from Me there?"

There are people who ask the question, "If God rules over the entire universe, how can He pay attention to me? How can He maintain His attention over every single individual in all creation?"

We must understand that just as God Himself is infinite, so is His intellect unbounded. A human mind may be able to concentrate on only one thing at a time. God, however, has no such restrictions. He can be aware of an infinite number of things, happening in an infinite number of places, all with one glance. God can maintain His gaze on the uncountable stars and galaxies of the universe, knowing exactly what is happening on each and every one of them at all times. There is not a single atom in all creation that escapes His constant scrutiny. This is what the Psalmist is teaching us when he sings "He numbers the stars and calls them all by name . . . His understanding is infinite" (*Psalms 147:4,5*). We may not be able to conceive of infinite understanding, but this is but another thing about God that is too deep for our grasp. The prophet thus tells us "no man can fathom His understanding" (*Isaiah 40:28*).

Beyond man's deeds, God scrutinizes the very convolutions of our brains and gazes at the depths of our souls. He not only knows our deeds, but also our very thoughts. The human mind was also created by God, and it lies open and transparent before Him. The Psalmist tells us of this when he chants (*Psalms 33:13–15*):

> God looks down from heaven,
> He sees the whole human race;
> From His place He watches,
> Probing all who live on earth.
> He has molded every heart together,
> He knows what each one does.

Even the innermost secrets of our hearts are thus open before God. The Psalmist speaks of this when he says "He knows the secrets of the heart" (*Ibid. 44:22*). He repeats this again, exclaiming "He knows the thoughts of man" (*Ibid 94:11*). For there are things in creation that are much more hidden than even man's thoughts, and these are nevertheless revealed before God. There are many secrets that only He knows, and in comparison, man's thoughts are a simple thing to probe. The wise Solomon thus declared "The pit and destruction lie open before God, how much more so, the hearts of man" (*Proverbs 15:11*).

It is impossible to fool God. He not only knows our actions, but also our motives. God Himself told His prophet "I, God, search the heart" (*Jeremiah 17:10*). The Prophet reiterates these words, saying "God . . . probes the heart" (*Ibid. 20:12*). These were also the words of the prophet Samuel, who said "Man looks at appearances, but God looks at the heart" (*I Samuel 16:7*).

A man might even fool himself, but God cannot be tricked. He not only knows our conscious motives, but even the depths of our unconscious. The wise Solomon taught us "A man's ways may strike him as pure, but God weighs the spirit" (*Proverbs 16:2*).

A person cannot think of anything or even begin to plan it, before God knows what is in his mind. One cannot hide even his most secret thoughts from God. This is what King David told his son Solomon "God searches every heart and knows every plan that it devises" (*I Chronicles 28:9*). Our sages comment on this: "Before a man speaks, God knows what is in his heart."[92] Another Midrash explains this even further:[93]

> Before a thought is formed in a man's heart, it is already revealed to God. Rabbi Yodin said in Rabbi Isaac's name, "Before it even begins to take form."

Just as God fills all space, He also fills all time. As we discussed earlier, God knows the future just as He knows the past and present.[94] We cannot comprehend time at all, and therefore, cannot fully understand how this is possible. Only God can see the future with absolute clarity, as He Himself told His prophet "I am God: There is none like Me, who can declare the end from the beginning. From ancient times, I reveal what is to be" (*Isaiah 46:9,10*).

God knew the destiny of the entire universe even before it was created. He knows every man's life even before he is born. He thus told His prophet "Before I formed you in the womb, I knew you" (*Jeremiah 1:5*). Our sages therefore teach us, "God knows man's thoughts even before there is any thought of creating him."[95]

The Psalmist also sang of this in the 139th Psalm that we quoted earlier. Here he speaks of how God knew his entire destiny even before he was born (*Psalm 139:15,16*):

> My bones were not hidden from You
>> When I was formed in secret,
>> Woven in the depths of the womb.
> You saw my unformed substance,
>> It was all written in Your book.
> My days were listed and determined,
>> Before the first one was even formed.

In order to give us free will, God must, to some extent, restrict His knowledge of the future. As we shall see, there are many ways in which God restricts Himself, especially with regard to His knowledge. For example, in a sense, God restricts Himself from seeing evil, as the Prophet exclaims "Your eyes are too pure to look upon evil, You cannot gaze upon wrongdoing . . ." (*Habakkuk 1:13*). [96]

It may be difficult to understand how God can know everything, yet at the same time restrict His gaze from seeing evil, but this is only one of the many ways where our limited intellect cannot comprehend the divine. One can also say that although God really knows the future, He restricts this knowledge when dealing with man. The Talmud thus teaches us, "God knows the future, but only judges man according to the present." [97]

This idea is expressed most clearly in a story brought in the Midrash: [98]

Just before the flood, the Torah tells us that, "God regretted that He had made man on the earth, and it grieved His heart" (*Genesis 6:6*). The Midrash discusses this paradox in terms of an anecdote.

A Roman was once conversing with Rabbi Joshua ben Korcha. He asked, "Do you not say that God knows the future?"

When the Rabbi replied in the affirmative, the Roman pressed the question further, "But it is written that God regretted that He made man and was grieved in His heart. Did He not know what man would end up doing?"

Rabbi Joshua responded by asking the Roman, "Do you have any children?"

When the Roman replied that he had several sons, Rabbi Joshua asked, "What did you do when they were born? Did you rejoice or did you mourn?"

"I rejoiced and made a great celebration," replied the Roman.

The sage pressed the point, "But why did you not mourn? Did you not know for sure that the child would eventually die? There is no man who can escape death."

The Roman answered, "Mourning is for the time of sadness. But in a time of joy we rejoice."

Rabbi Joshua replied, "That answers your question. The same is true of God."

Rabbi Joshua was really giving the Roman a very profound answer. He taught him that a person can know something beyond the shadow of a doubt, and yet ignore this knowledge completely. One knows for certain that a newborn child will eventually die, but still, he ignores this fact and rejoices in the child's birth. If man can ignore certain knowledge, how much more so is this possible for God. God's power is infinite, not only to do, but also to restrict Himself in order to make creation follow His plan.

14.

The final thing that we know about God is that He is absolutely hidden. Not only can we not see God with our eyes, but even our minds are inadequate to the task of perceiving Him.

The Torah speaks of this when Moses asked God to let him perceive His glory. He asked God "I beseech You, let me behold Your glory" (Exodus 33:18). God answered him "You cannot see My face, for no man can see Me and live" (Ibid. 33:20). If a man were to see God, he would absolutely cease to exist. There might be a prophetic vision or symbol, but God Himself cannot be seen. [99]

This is well illustrated by the following Midrashic anecdote: [100]

King Androninos once was having a conversation with Rabbi Joshua. He asked, "Is there a Master of the world?"

"Is the world then without meaning or purpose?" countered the Rabbi.

When the king asked Rabbi Joshua who was this Master and Creator, the Rabbi answered quite positively that it was God.

The king looked a bit puzzled. He said to the sage, "I am a king. It would be ridiculous for me never to show myself to my subjects. They would forget me completely. Why doesn't God reveal Himself once or twice a year, so that people would see and fear Him?"

The Rabbi answered, "God does not reveal Himself because no man could bear His glory. Is it not written, 'no man can see Me and live'?"

The king insisted and said, "If you do not show me your God, I will not believe that He exists."

Rabbi Joshua replied, "Very well. If you really want to see God, look up and gaze at the summer sun."

"But who can possibly gaze at the sun?" exclaimed the monarch.

The Rabbi smiled and said, "Listen to your own words. The sun is only one of God's vast multitude of servants. Still, no man can gaze at it. But God's glory fills the universe. How could a mere mortal possibly gaze at it?"

Rabbi Joshua is teaching us an important lesson about why we cannot see God. This lesson is really deeper than it might appear at first glance. It is telling us that God cannot reveal Himself because man could no more exist in the presence of God's glory than in the center of the sun. Existence itself is merely a mirror of God's power. In God's presence, it would be like sunlight inside of the sun. The light would have absolutely no independent existence. In the same manner, if God were to reveal Himself, then there would not be able to be any independent existence in all creation. [101] Our sages teach us, "What good is a torch in broad daylight?" [102] Existence in God's presence would be less than the light of a candle in the center of the sun.

As we discussed in the previous section, one of God's great powers is that of restricting Himself. If a human being can restrict himself, we cannot say less about God. The prophet thus speaks to God and says "You are a God who hides Himself" (Isaiah 45:15). The Psalmist sings "He dwells in the highest mystery, He rests in the shadow of Shadai" (Psalms 91:1). The Midrash explains this verse by saying, "The Holy One dwells in the shadow of the world. He sees all and yet is unseen." [103]

Since it is God Who hides Himself, no one can in any way uncover Him. Elihu told this to Job when he said "When He hides His face, who can behold Him?" (*Job 34:29*).

We cannot perceive or comprehend God both because He is too close and because He is too far. God has given man the ability to understand the world, but man's power does not extend beyond that. There is a limit beyond which man's intellect can no longer function, and God's realm lies far beyond that limit. The wise Solomon taught us this lesson when he said "He has permitted man to consider the world, but man cannot comprehend the work of God from the beginning to the end" (*Ecclesiastes 3:11*).

Man's intellect can soar beyond the stars and to the far reaches past the stars. But his mind is still limited by his physical nature. This was the lesson that Eliphaz the Yemenite taught Job when he said "God is in the zenith of the heavens. He looks down at the stars, high as they are" (*Job 22:12*).

To reach God would be like trying to remember before your existence. It would be like trying to recall your existence in your mother's womb, before your very mind came into being. No thought symbols exist in our minds to even begin to handle such things. Here again, we see Solomon's wisdom declaring "As you remember not the way your spirit and bones grew in the womb, neither can you know the work of God, Who is behind it all" (*Ecclesiastes 11:5*).

One can keep on counting forever and not reach infinity. One can probe to the very limits of intellect and never reach the infinite God. Were man to fathom the deepest mysteries of all creation, he would not even reach the outskirts of God's true greatness.

Job speaks of this. He tells of all the unknowable mysteries of creation and dispairs of ever even being able to peer deeper than through the shallowest surface of these mysteries. Then, after speaking of these mysteries, he says "These are but the fringes of His power, a faint whisper that we hear of Him. But who can fathom the thunder of His might?" (*Job 26:15*).

What Job is saying is that all that we can comprehend is like the merest whisper, while in comparison, God's power is like the loudest thunder. Elihu echoes these same words to

Job, "With His voice, God thunders wondrously. He does great things that we cannot understand" (*Ibid. 37:5*). Again, he says "God's greatness exceeds our knowledge, the number of His years is beyond computing" (*Ibid. 36:26*). There is no way that we can grasp the infinite.

Another one of Job's friends expresses the utter hopelessness of ever attempting to probe the depths of the Divine. He speaks to Job and tells him (*Ibid. 11:7-9*):

> Can you probe the depths of God?
> Can you fathom Almighty's mystery?
> It is higher than heaven, what can you do?
> Deeper than deep, what can you know?
> Longer than the earth is its measure,
> And broader than the sea.

The idea of God's total transcendence and the impossibility of understanding Him is best expressed by Elijah, who says to God in his introduction to the *Tikuney Zohar*: "No thought can grasp You at all." [104] Rabbi Schneur Zalman of Liadi, the founder of Chabad, interprets this by saying, "Just as a physical hand cannot grasp a thought, so too, man's intellect cannot grasp God." [105] God is a dimension even beyond thought. Our minds may reach out to Him, but can no more grasp Him than our hands can grasp a thought. [106]

We come to God with faith and prayer rather than with true understanding. Ultimately, all we know about God is what He Himself revealed to us. Beyond that, God is totally beyond the reach of the human intellect. He is hidden, not only from our sight, but also from our minds. We might reach up to grasp a star, but our hands would never even come close to touching one. The same is true of God. He Himself tells us this, when He speaks to His prophet and says (*Isiah 55:8,9*):

> My thoughts are not your thoughts,
> My ways are not your ways . . .
> As the heavens are higher than the earth
> So are My ways higher than yours
> And My thoughts above your thoughts.

# # # # # # #

NOTES

PART ONE: FOUNDATIONS

1 *Cf. Mesilath Yesharim* 1.
2 *Zohar Chadash* 70d. *Cf. Avoth* 3:1.
3 *Yad, Yesodey HaTorah* 1:1–5.
4 Also see Psalm 53:2.
5 *Moreh Nevuchim* 1:44.
6 *Chovoth HaLevavoth* 1:6 end.
7 *Bereshith Rabbah* 39:1.
8 *Zohar* 1:2a.
9 *Chovoth HaLevavoth* 2:5; *Pardes Rimonim* 8:1; *Shnei Luchoth HaB'rith (Shaar HaGadol)*, Jerusalem 5720, 1:46b. *Cf. Bereshith Rabbah* 48:2.
10 *Tanchuma, Toldos* 5.
11 *VeHi SheAmdah*, in Passover Hagaddah.
12 *Sifri* (346) on Deuteronomy 33:5, *Midrash Tehillim* 123:2; *Pesikta* 12 (102b); *Yalkut* 1:275, 2:317; Abarbanel *ad loc.*
13 See *Targum J., Mechilta* on Exodus 12:37.
14 *Yad, Yesodey HaTorah* 8:1; *Kuzari* 1:87.
15 Ramban *ad loc*, and on Additions to *Sefer HaMitzvoth*, negative commandment #2; *Sefer Mitzvoth Gadol (Smag)*, negative commandment #13.
16 *Moreh Nevuchim* 2:35.
17 Ramban *loc. cit.* #1, quoting *Halakhoth Gedoloth*. Cf. *Sefer Mitzvoth Gadol*, negative commandment #64.
18 This is repeated in Deuteronomy 5:6.
19 Ibn Ezra, Ramban, *ad loc.*; *Kuzari* 1:25; *Chinuch* 25.
20 *Cf. Kuzari* 1:1,2. See also Ezekiel 8:12, 9:9.
21 Exodus 15:2.
22 See *Likutey Halakhoth (Yoreh Deah) Shavuoth* 2:2.
23 *Cf. VaYikra Rabbah* 28:1; *Targum J.* on Genesis 4:8.

[24] *Cf. Avoth* 4:11, 5:17.

[25] *Yad, Yesodey HaTorah* 1:6; *Sefer HaMitzvoth*, positive commandment #1; *Sefer Mitzvoth Gadol*, positive #1; *Zohar* 2:25a, 3:256b. See also Josephus, *Antiquities* 3:5:5, who also appears to concur with this opinion. *Cf. Makkoth* 24a.

[26] *Chinuch* 25. This may also answer the objection of the Ramban, quoted in the following note. However, the Ramban might counter by placing this in the category of remembering rather than believing. See note 17.

[27] Ramban on *Sefer HaMitzvoth, loc. cit.* See also *Halachoth Gedoloth* and *Sefer HaMitzvoth* of Rabbi Saadia Gaon, who also omit it.

[28] *Yad, Yesodey HaTorah* 1:6; *Sefer HaMitzvoth*, negative commandment #1; *Sefer Mitzvoth Gadol*, negative 1.

[29] *Chinuch* 26.

[30] *Kiddushin* 40a; *Yerushalmi Nazir* 4:3 (17a); *Tosefta Nazir* 3:6, from Ezekiel 14:5. *Cf.* Radak ad loc. *Zohar* 2:150b.

[31] *Sefer Mitzvoth Gadol*, loc. cit. See *Mekhilta* and Ibn Ezra on Exodus 22:19. *Cf.* 2 Kings 17:33, and Rashi and Radak on Judges 10:6, from *Pethicha Eicha Rabbah* 10, *Betza* 25b.

[32] *Yad, Avodath Kochavim* 1:1; *Moreh Nevukhim* 1:36.

[33] *Thirteen Principles of Faith* #5.

[34] *Sanhedrin* 7:6 (60b); Ramban on Exodus 20:3.

[35] *Sanhedrin* 63a; *Succah* 45b; *Yad, Shavuoth* 11:2.

[36] *Yad, Melakhim* 9:3.

[37] See *Yad, loc. cit.*, which states that a non-Jew is only liable for those types of idolatry for which a Jew incurs a death penalty, *cf. Minchath Chinukh* 26:6. However, this only involves the *deed* of idolatry, *cf. Sanhedrin* 63a; *Yad, Avodath Kochavim* 3:4.

[38] See *Tosafoth, Bekhoroth* 2b s.v. "*Sh'ma;*" *Sanhedrin* 63b, s.v. "*Asur;*" *Orach Chaim* 156:1 in *Hagah; Rosh, Sanhedrin* 7:3, *Pilpula Charifta ad loc.; Darkey Moshe, Yoreh Deah* 151; *Shach ibid.* 151:7; *Mach'tzith HaShekel, Orach Chaim* 156:2; *Teshuvoth Tashbatz* 1:139; *Teshuvoth VeShev HaKohen* 38; *Mishnath Chakhamim* on *Yad, Yesodey HaTorah*, quoted in *Pithchey Teshuvah, Yoreh Deah* 147:2; Maharatz Chayoth on *Horioth* 8b. There is another opinion that this is only forbidden in the land of Israel, *cf.* Maharatz Chayoth on *Berakhoth* 57a; Ramban

on Leviticus 18:25; Rabbi Yaakov Emden, *Mor U'Ketzia* 224.

39 *Cf.* Rashbam *ad loc.*; *Derech Mitzvothekha* (Chabad) p. 59b.

40 *Cf. Kuzari* 4:23; Rambam, end of Halkhoth Melachim (Amsterdam, 1702), quoted in Ramban, *Torath HaShem Temimah*, in *Kithvey Ramban*, Jerusalem, 5723, p. 1:144; *Teshuvoth Rambam* 58; *Teshuvoth Rivash* 119; *Akedath Yitzchok* 88.

41 *Teshuvoth Nodeh BeYehudah, Yoreh Deah*, end of 2:148; *Teshuvoth Meil Tzadakah* 22; *Teshuvoth Shaar Ephraim* 24; all quoted in *Pithchey Teshuvah, Yoreh Deah* 147:2; *Pri Megadim, Eshel Avraham* 156:2, *Sifethey Daath* (*Yoreh Deah*) 65:11); *Chatham Sofer* on *Orach Chaim* 156:1; *Minchath Chinukh* 86.

42 *Makkoth* 24a. However, see *Shir HaShirim Rabbah* 1:13, where we find an opinion that disputes this and maintains that all Ten Commandments were given directly at Sinai. See Ramban on Exodus 20:7, and on *Sefer HaMitzvoth, Shoresh* #1. Also see *Pirkey DeRabbi Eliezer* 41, Radal *ad loc.* 41:77; *Sh'moth Rabbah* 42:7. In *Moreh Nevukhim* 2:33, we find that the very fact of revelation demonstrated these two commandments. See also *Kol Yehudah* on *Kuzari* 1:87 (52b) s.v. "VeEleh."

43 *Moreh Nevukhim loc. cit.*; Rashi, *Makkoth* 22a s.v. "MiPi."

44 *Yad, Yesodey HaTorah* 1:6; *Avodath Kokhavim* 2:4; *Kiddushin* 40a.

45 *Tosefta Shavuoth* 3:5.

46 Ramban *ad loc.*; Abarbanel on *Moreh* 2:31.

47 *Moreh Nevukhim* 2:31, 3:32, 3:41; *Sefer HaChinukh* 32; Ibn Ezra, Bachya, on Exodus 20:8; Ramban on Deuteronomy 5:15; *Menorath HaMaor* 159; *Akedath Yitzchok* 4, 55; *Sh'nei Luchoth HaB'rith* (*Mesekhta Shabbath*) 2:10b. Cf. *Mekhilta* on Exodus 31:14.

48 *Moreh Nevukhim* 1:34; Radak on 1 Chronicles 28:29.

49 *Cf.* Kuzari 1:114, 4:13.

50 *Cf.* Ibn Ezra on Proverbs 30:19.

51 *Sifra* and Rashi on Leviticus 26:15; *Yalkut* 1:673.

52 *Cf. Pesachim* 59b; *Nazir* 23b; *Yoreh Deah* 146:20.

53 Reading of *Reshith Chakhmah, Shaar HaTeshuvah* #7 (New York, 5728) 123c, of *Yerushalmi Chaggigah* 1:7

(6b). See *Pethichta Eicha Rabbah* 2; *Pesikta* 15 (121a); *Yalkut* 2:282.

54 See note 17.
55 See Rashi, Radak *ad loc.*; *Moreh Nevukhim* 3:51,52; *Orach Chaim* 1:1 in *Hagah. Cf. Sanhedrin* 22a; *Reshith Chachmah, Shaar HaYira* 1 (8d).

PART TWO: GOD

1 *Megillah* 31a.
2 *Sotah* 5a.
3 See *Emunoth VeDeyoth* 1:1; *Yad, Yesodey HaTorah* 1:1, 1:5; *Mechilta* on Exodus 6:2 (120a); *Sifra* on Leviticus 18:2 (85c).
4 *Metzudoth, Targum ad loc.; Reshith Chakhmah* 1:1 (9c).
5 *Yad, Teshuvah* 3:7, Raavad *ad loc.*; Ramban on Genesis 1:1; *Emunoth VeDeyoth* 5:8 (74a); *Kuzari* 1:67 (41a).
6 *Bereshith Rabbah* 1:12. See Raavad *loc. cit.*
7 Alluding to the things mentioned in Genesis 1:2. According to the Ramban ad loc., the philosopher was referring to the primeval matter of the Hyle, the primitive Form, and the four elements of the ancient world, fire, air, water, and dust. See also *Torath HaShem Temimah* p. 156.
8 Ramban on Genesis 1:3. Also see *Kuzari* 4:25 (44a). *Cf. Midrash Tehillim* 107:3.
9 *Bereshith Rabbah* 12:10, 4:7.
10 *Minachoth* 29b; Rashi on Genesis 2:4. See also *Etz Yosef* on *Bereshith Rabbah* 12:10.
11 Ramban *loc. cit., Moreh Nevukhim* 1:66.
12 *Magid Devarav LeYaakov* 102.
13 *Cf.* Jeremiah 51:15.
14 Ramban on Genesis 1:1, *Thirteen Principles of Faith* #1, *Yad, Teshuvah* 3:7.
15 See *Targum ad loc.*
16 See Malbim, *Metzudoth ad loc.*
17 *Yerushalmi Berakhoth* 1:5 (9b); *VaYikra Rabbah* 26:1. See Rashi, Radak *ad loc.*; *Yad, Yesodey HaTorah* 1:4.
18 *Shabbath* 55a.

19 See also Psalm 10:16, 29:10, 146:10.
20 *Chovoth HaLevavoth* 1:10 (Warsaw 5635) p. 40a; *Moreh Nevukhim* 1:58; *Kuzari* 2:2; *Ikkarim* 2:22.
21 *Midrash Tehillim* 103:4, according to reading and interpretation of *Shomer Emunim* (*HaKadmon*) 2:9–11. For other versions and readings, see *Berakhoth* 10a; *VaYikra Rabbah* 4:8; *Devarim Rabbah* 2:26; *Pirkey DeRabbi Eliezer* 34; *Tikuney Zohar* 13 (28a). See also *Derech HaShem* #1.
22 See *Iyun Yaakov* on *Berakhoth* 10a (in *Eyn Yaakov* #50).
23 *Thirteen Principles of Faith* #2; *Yad, Teshuvah* 3:7.
24 *Yad, Avodath Kochavim* 1; *Daath Tevunah* (Rabbi Moshe Chaim Luzzato, Tel Aviv, 5726) p. 13.
25 *Daath Tevunah loc. cit.* See also *Sifri HaAzinu* #329. *Cf.* *Berakhoth* 33b.
26 See *Pardes Rimonim* 2:7; *Shefa Tal* 1:3.
27 *Thirteen Principles of Faith* #3; *Yad, Teshuvah* 3:6, Raavad *ad loc.*; *Iggereth Techiyath HaMethim* p. 4; *Ikkarim* 1:2, 2:7; *Pardes Rimonim* 1:9.
28 See *Chovoth HaLevavoth* 1:10 (41b); *Yad, Yesodey HaTorah* 1:8, 1:11, from *Chagigah* 15a; *Moreh Nevukhim* 1:35, 2:1 end; *Kuzari* 5:18 #6.
29 *Chovoth HaLevavoth* 39b; *Moreh Nevukhim* 1:58; *Pardes Rimonim* 3:1, 4:8; *Ikkarim* 2:22. See also *Zohar* 2:42b; *Nefesh HaChaim* 2:2.
30 *Mekhilta* (65a), Rashi on Exodus 19:18; *Tanchuma Yithro* 13; *Bereshith Rabbah* 27:1; *Koheleth Rabbah* 2:24; *Pesikta* 4 (36b); *Moreh Nevuchim* 1:26, 1:47; *Emunoth VeDeyoth* 2:10; *Chovoth HaLevavoth* 1:10; *Kuzari* 4:3 (18a). See also Ramban on Genesis 46:1; *Tifereth Yisrael* (Maharal) 33.
31 *Berakhoth* 31b and parallels; *Sifra* on Leviticus 20:2; *Yad, Yesodey HaTorah* 1:12; *Chovoth HaLevavoth loc. cit.*
32 *Cf.* Exodus 24:10.
33 *Yad, loc. cit.*
34 *Tikuney Zohar* 17a.
35 *Nefesh HaChaim* 1:1; *Pardes Rimonim* 31:8; *Etz Chaim, Drush Egolim VaYashar* 5; *Shomer Emunim* (*HaKadmon*) 1:25.
36 *Zohar* 1:90b, 2:96b, 3:71b; *Likutey Amarim* (*Tanya*) 1:4.
37 *Tana DeBei Eliahu Rabbah*, end of #1.
38 *Kuzari* 4:3, *Tosafoth, Kiddushin* 3b, s.v. "*DeAsar.*" See also Leviticus 19:2, 21:8, Isaiah 6:3; *VaYikra Rabbah* 24:9.

[39] *Emunoth VeDeyoth* 1:4.

[40] *Midrash Tehillim* 103:5.

[41] *Chagigah* 13b.

[42] *Emunoth VeDeyoth* 2:11,12, *Sh'vil Emunah ad loc*. #10; *Moreh Nevukhim* 2:13, 2:30; *Ikkarim* 2:18; *Pardes Rimonim* 3:1, 4:7; *Torath HaOlah* (Isserles) 3:59; *Yaaroth Devash* on *Megillah* 9a; *Asarah Maamaros* 1:16; *Derech Mitzvothekha* (Chabad) 57a. Also see *Bereshith Rabbah* 3:8.

[43] *Pardes Rimonim* 6:3.

[44] *Bereshith Rabbah* 68:10; *Sh'moth Rabbah* 45:6; *Midrash Tehillim* 50; *Pesikta Rabathai* 21 (104b); *Yalkut* 2:841; Radak on Psalm 90:1; *Nefesh HaChaim* 3:1–3.

[45] *Cf.* Rashi, *Baaley Tosafoth ad loc*.

[46] *Ibid. Cf.* Radak *ad loc*.

[47] See note 42. Also see Albert Einstein, *Relativity, the Special and General Theory* (Crown, New York, 1961), Appendix 5.

[48] *Sanhedrin* 38a; *Yerushalmi Sanhedrin* 4:9 (23b); *Bereshith Rabbah* 8:5.

[49] See also Psalm 22:10, 102:13.

[50] *Yebamoth* 16b. See also *Yad, Yesodey HaTorah* 1:10; *Emunoth VeDeyoth* 2:10; *Kuzari* 5:18 #5; *Ikkarim* 2:19. *Cf. Bereshith Rabbah* 81:2; *Mekhilta* on Exodus 22:3 (67b); *VaYikra Rabbah* 19:2 end; Ibn Ezra on Ecclesiastes 3:15.

[51] *Cheredim* #5 (Jerusalem, 5718) p. 42; *Elemah Rabathai* 1:1:15.

[52] *Emunoth VeDeyoth*, end of #1; *Shomer Emunim (HaKadmon)* 2:17. *Cf. Etz Chaim, Drush Egolim VeYashar* #1.

[53] *Shnei Luchoth HaB'rith, Beth HaShem* 1:6a, note; *Cheredim* #5 (p. 40).

[54] *Yad, Yesodey HaTorah* 1:11; *Moreh Nevuchim* 1:54; *Emunoth VeDeyoth* 2:11; *Ikkarim* 2:14.

[55] *Bereshith Rabbah* 81:2.

[56] See above, note 18.

[57] *Ikkarim* 2:27.

[58] See Rabbi Moshe Almosnino, *Pirkey Moshe*, quoted in *Midrash Shmuel* and *Tosafoth Yom Tov* on *Avoth* 3:15; *Yesod Emunah* (Rabbi Baruch Kasover) 2; *Sh'vil Emunah* (on *Emunoth VeDeyoth*) 4:4:11. Also see *Kol Yehudah*

(on *Kuzari*) 5:20 (47b); *Otzar Nechemad* (on *Kuzari*) 1:1 (11b), s.v. "*Kol.*"

Rosh HaShanah 18a. See Rambam, *Tosafoth Yom Tov Ibid.* 1:2.

60 *Pesikta* 6 (57b).

61 *Yad, Yesodey HaTorah* 2:3; *Moreh Nevuchim* 3:13; *Emunoth VeDeyoth* 1:4, *Sh'vil Emunah ad loc.* 1:4:9; *Reshith Chachmah* 1:1 (8d).

62 See *VaYikra Rabbah* 4:8; *Midrash Sh'muel* 5.

63 See Ramban on Deuteronomy 22:6; *Sefer HaChinukh* 545; *Nefesh HaChaim* 2:4. *Cf.* Radak on Psalm 16:2.

64 *Bereshith Rabbah* 44:1; *VaYikra Rabbah* 13:3; *Tanchuma Shemini* 8; *Midrash Tehillim* 18:25; *Yalkut* 2:121; *Moreh Nevuchim* 3:26; *Avodath HaKodesh* 2:3; *Shnei Luchoth HaBrith, Shaar HaGadol* (1:48b); *Tifereth Yisrael* (Maharal) 7.

65 *Yerushalmi Nedarim* 9:1 (29a).

66 *VaYikra Rabbah* 27:2; *BaMidbar Rabbah* 14:2; *Tanchuma Kedoshim* 16.

67 See *Zohar* 2:274a.

68 *Zohar* 3:225a; *Likutey Amarim* (*Tanya*) 2:7 (83b); *Nefesh HaChaim* 3:4; *Reshith Chachmah* 1:1 (9a).

69 *Shnei Luchoth HaBrith* 1:44a, 1:64b; *Likutey Amarim* (*Tanya*) 84a.

70 *Berachoth* 12a; *Zohar* 3:272b.

71 *Cf. Sifri ad loc.* #31.

72 *Ibid.*

73 *Zohar Chadash, Yithro* 35c.

74 *BaMidbar Rabbah* 12:4; *Pesikta* 1 (2b).

75 *Midrash Tehillim* 24:5.

76 *Kuzari* 1:79 (47a), 1:98 (66b), 2:46 (54b) 3:23 (31b).

77 *Berachoth* 6a; *Avoth* 3:5.

78 *Sanhedrin* 39a.

79 Ibn Ezra on Exodus 13:21; *Emunoth VeDeyoth* 2:11; *Kuzari* 2:7,8; *Moreh Nevukhim* 1:27; Ramban on Genesis 47:1.

80 *Mechilta* on Exodus 13:21 (25a).

81 *Taanith* 21b.

82 *Succah* 53a, according to Rashi.

83 *Kiddushin* 31a.

84 See *Pardes Rimonim* 6:8; *Likutey Amarim* (*Tanya*) 2:2 (77b).

68

[85] See *Metzudoth ad loc.; Tosafoth Yom Tov* on *Tamid* 7:4 s.v. *"LeChayay."*
[86] *Zohar* 2:42b; *Tikuney Zohar* 3a, 62a; *Reshith Chochmah* 7a, 8c,d; Radak on Jeremiah 23:24.
[87] *Shomer Emunim (HaKadmon)* 2:11.
[88] *Midrash Tehillim* 119:36.
[89] *Thirteen Principles of Faith* #10.
[90] *Tanchuma Nasa* 5; *Yalkut* 2:305.
[91] See *Yerushalmi Rosh HaShanah* 1:3 (8a).
[92] *Sh'moth Rabbah* 21:3.
[93] *Bereshith Rabbah* 9:3.
[94] *Sanhedrin* 90b.
[95] *Tanna DeBei Eliahu Zuta* 23 (50b).
[96] *Elemah Rabathai* 1:2:18; *Or HaChaim* on Genesis 6:6; *Meshekh Chakhmah* on Genesis 1:26.
[97] *Yerushalmi Rosh HaShanah* 1:3 (7b).
[98] *Bereshith Rabbah* 27:7.
[99] *Sifri*, Rashi, on Numbers 12:8.
[100] *Yalkut* 1:396. *Cf. Chulin* 60a.
[101] *Shefa Tal*, Introduction (4d); *Likutey Amarim (Tanya)* 2:6 (81a).
[102] *Chulin* 60b. *Cf. Zohar* 3:47b.
[103] *BaMidbar Rabbah* 12:3.
[104] *Tikuney Zohar* 17a.
[105] *Likutey Amarim (Tanya)* 2:9 (86b).
[106] *Cf. Chagigah* 13b; *Yad, Yesodey HaTorah* 2:8.